Getting Started in

Internet Investing

The Getting Started In Series

Getting Started in Online Day Trading by Kassandra Bentley
Getting Started in Asset Allocation by Bill Bresnan and Eric P. Gelb
Getting Started in Online Investing by David L. Brown and Kassandra Bentley
Getting Started in Stocks by Alvin D. Hall
Getting Started in Mutual Funds by Alvin D. Hall
Getting Started in Estate Planning by Kerry Hannon
Getting Started in Online Personal Finance by Brad Hall
Getting Started in 401(k) Investing by Paul Katzeff
Getting Started in Internet Investing by Paul Katzeff
Getting Started in Security Analysis by Peter J. Klein
Getting Started in Global Investing by Robert Kreitler
Getting Started in Futures by Todd Lofton
Getting Started in Financial Information by Daniel Moreau and Tracey Longo
Getting Started in Technical Analysis by Jack D. Schwager
Getting Started in Hedge Funds by Daniel A. Strachman
Getting Started in Options by Michael C. Thomsett
Getting Started in Real Estate Investing by Michael C. Thomsett and Jean Freestone Thomsett
Getting Started in Annuities by Gordon M. Williamson
Getting Started in Bonds by Sharon Saltzgiver Wright
Getting Started in Retirement Planning by Ronald M. Yolles and Murray Yolles

Getting Started in

Internet Investing

Paul Katzeff

John Wiley & Sons, Inc.

New York • Chichester • Weinheim • Brisbane • Singapore • Toronto

This book is printed on acid-free paper. ∞

Published by John Wiley & Sons, Inc.
Published simultaneously in Canada.

Library of Congress Cataloging-in-Publication Data:
Katzeff, Paul, 1948–
Getting started in Internet investing / Paul Katzeff
p.cm.—(Getting started in)
Includes index.
ISBN 0-471-39681-8 (pbk. : alk. paper)
1. Internet industry—Finance. 2. Investments. I. Title. II. Series.

HD9696.8.A2 K38 2001
332.63'22–dc21 2001017502

Printed in the United States of America

10 9 8 7 6 5 4 3 2 1

Acknowledgments

I owe thanks to many people who were generous with their time and expertise. In particular, I would like to thank money managers and financial professionals Catherine Baker of RS Investment Management, Jason Burr of MAXfunds, Paul Cook of Munder Capital Management, Peter Doyle of Kinetics Asset Management, Mark Herskovitz of Dreyfus, Ryan Jacob of Jacob Asset Management, Robert Markman of Markman MultiFunds, and Bryan Olson of Charles Schwab & Co. I'm also grateful to firms that provided data and other information: Forrester Research, International Data, Jupiter Research, Lipper, MAXfunds, Media Metrix, Morgan Stanley Dean Witter, and U.S. Bancorp Piper Jaffray. In addition, editor Doug Rogers provided savvy input.

Certainly, this book could not have been written without the encouragement of my friends and family. Also, I want to thank Debra Englander of John Wiley & Sons for her patience. And, of course, special thanks to Janet for making this part of her life.

P. K.

Contents

Introduction

TAPPING INTO FUTURE GROWTH

As fast as you can click a computer mouse, the Internet has evolved from geek gizmo to mainstream tool.

You've used it to send and receive business memos, give and get casual e-mail. Kids use it to research their homework; adults use it to book airline tickets, check the weather, read the news, track Wall Street.

Increasingly, people log on to buy and sell stocks. Ever-larger crowds of people bid on bejeweled bracelets at online auctions. And growing numbers of neighbors visit—*ahem*—adult-content sites, according to the people who count such things.

It is a mirror of our entire society.

It is a social center and a shopping mall.

Like an electronic version of the backyard fence, it is a place where we chat and gossip.

Like a plugged-in downtown USA, it is zoned for business.

No wonder it has become one other thing as well: the source of enormous new wealth. Here's how:

In 1995, only two companies that are now considered Internet businesses by most head counts had shares that members of the public could buy and sell on an open stock exchange.

By the end of 1998, there were still only 88 publicly traded companies in this exotic, new business category. All combined, their stock was worth $364 billion, says the investment firm U.S. Bancorp Piper Jaffray.

Just one year later, the Net's population had exploded to 279 companies. Collectively they were worth $1.3 trillion.

Even after the notorious retreat by technology stocks in the spring of 2000, by the summer of 2000, 399 Internet companies had climbed back up to nearly $1 trillion in value, says Morgan Stanley Dean Witter. And that doesn't even count seven colossal corporations, including Cisco Systems, Sun Microsystems, and America Online, which Morgan Stanley puts into an overlapping pigeonhole it calls *Internet-related*. Tally in those giants and the collective price tag for Internet stocks soars to $2.45 trillion.

That increase of more than $1 *trillion* in 18 months isn't a mere economist's abstraction. It is real money. It is the growth in wealth enjoyed by people who owned stock in those companies.

Who are those shareholders? People throughout those firms: chief executives, middle managers, secretaries. It is also owned by shrewd outside investors who provided startup cash for those businesses. And it is owned by day-trading grad students at MIT and Cal Tech, who first read about those firms in technical journals.

You too may already be a shareholder, either by owning stock directly or through the mutual funds in your 401(k) plan, for example.

"The Internet is the biggest investment development in our lifetimes," says Bryan Olson, Director of megabrokerage Charles Schwab's Center for Investment Research. "The short-term ups and downs of the Internet in the marketplace don't lessen its continuing impact."

Robert Markman, head of the Markman MultiFunds family of mutual funds and an investment strategist, adds, "This is just the second or third inning of a ball game that will go extra innings."

By way of elaboration, Markman says, "The Internet affects personal relationships and business relationships, and it does that all around the globe. It reduces the time it takes to exchange information and knowledge—whether that consists of saying hello to a friend, or exchanging data with a business. And anything that reduces the time it takes to get things done goes to the heart of corporate profitability. Even with occasional ups and downs, its impact is going to grow enormously."

Fan-tas-tic!

But if the Internet is such a big deal, and if such enormous wealth is erupting from it, why isn't everyone on the planet already a multibillionaire from investing in dot-com businesses?

For one thing, the Internet's downs have been as spectacular as its ups.

The year 2000 in particular was a downer for the Net. The ISDEX, an index that serves as a popular cross-section of the Internet, lost 58 percent in 2000, according to internet.com's Internet Stock Report. In fact, fewer than four percent of all Internet stocks posted gains during 2000, the web site reported.

So the days of seemingly automatic profits in the Internet are gone. Investors can no longer pick winners by throwing darts at a listing of stocks or funds. Yet every bull market starts from the rubble of a bear market. Many big winners will emerge from the Internet's setback in 2000. Investors, though, must choose stocks and funds carefully.

But even in the rosiest of market times, many investors are frozen by the fear. Afraid of making an investment mistake, too many do nothing instead.

Their worry now goes like this: Sure, there are some good Internet companies, but there are lots of dogs too. How do you know which ones will succeed in the long run? After all, we've been through a phase when the success of early Net companies lured many imitators. New competitors sprang up like weeds on a front lawn. But before long, there were too many firms selling weed killer online and not enough suburban yards.

Catherine Baker, comanager of the RS Internet Age Fund, says those people are worried about the wrong thing. "Some e-tailers are not doing great," she says. "Many will go bust. But that's business life. What you really should be afraid of if you're an investor is owning stock in a company that's *not* looking at how it can use the Internet. If you own stock in a business that isn't looking at how its competition can use the Internet to leapfrog them, then you're going to end up with a pile of stock certificates you can throw into the garbage."

Your challenge as an investor is to pick winners while avoiding losers. But you can't succeed by doing nothing. And that's the purpose of *Getting Started in Internet Investing*: helping you pick ways to invest in the Internet.

INTRODUCTION

The Internet is a very important technological development.

Its impact on business is probably the *most* important economic event of our day. It will continue to reshape the corporate landscape. It will continue to generate enormous wealth. It will continue to create huge opportunities.

But it will pose investment risks as well. Not all enterprises doing business online will flourish. Not all of the Internet's suppliers will either.

There's no easy way to foretell the winners and losers among the companies running e-mail services or auction sites, building backroom computers or the Internet's phone lines. So this book will explain:

- ✔ What the Internet is.
- ✔ What types of companies do business on the Internet.
- ✔ What types of companies make money helping to build, operate, and supply the Net.
- ✔ How to make investment decisions that reflect your unique needs and circumstances.
- ✔ How to pick Internet stocks.
- ✔ How to select a mutual fund that invests in the Internet.
- ✔ How to understand Internet jargon, which can be as confusing as an unfamiliar foreign language.

In fact, everything in *Getting Started in Internet Investing* will be explained in plain English. You won't need to be a computer systems analyst to understand this book's explanation of the Internet. You won't need a master's degree from Harvard Business School to understand our description of the various flavors of Internet businesses. You won't need a seat on the New York Stock Exchange to grasp our lessons on how to make investment decisions.

All you need is a healthy curiosity, and the pages of this book open in your hands.

Chapter 1

How the Internet Is an Investment Opportunity

Levi Strauss didn't make money panning for gold. He built his fortune peddling denim jeans to hordes of gold miners during California's Gold Rush.

The lesson for anyone trying to figure out how to invest in the Internet is that the key is the online population explosion. You don't need to be a software whiz or computer nerd to make money off Net mania.

It is the throngs of people flocking to use the Internet who create opportunities. Collectively, they make up a huge pool of shoppers, eagerly buying and selling all sorts of goods and services. They provide advertisers with a sizable audience. In their stampede to get online, they are buying new computers, software, and doodads like modems. To carry their calls, phone companies and cable TV firms are stringing millions of miles of fiber-optic cables. High-tech foundries race to fabricate enough computer chips for the innards of everything from cell phones to servers.

Server A computer that stores information and software programs and provides (or *serves*) them to people using other computers. A server is the host to groups of computers linked in a network.

BUILD IT, AND THEY WILL COME

You can invest in this cyberspace migration in whatever way best suits your temperament, checking account, time frame, and goals.

You can buy stock in companies that exploit this electronic revolution one at a time, like a sharpshooter picking off ducks in a carnival shooting gallery. Or you can invest in several at once—even in entire categories of businesses—like a fisherman casting a wide net.

Whichever approach you take, you'll be helped by the fact that the online population attracting all of these companies is growing as fast as the crowd filling a ballpark before the deciding game of the World Series.

Just look at the trends:

- ✔ The number of Americans using the Internet hit 107 million in 1999. That multitude soared to 137 million in the year 2000, the research firm International Data Corp. says.
- ✔ Business conducted worldwide over the Internet will balloon to $6.8 trillion by 2004. That's up from $657 billion now, as data from Forrester Research shows in Table. 1.1. How huge is $6.8 trillion? It's twice as big as China's whole economy was in the late 1990s.
- ✔ Consumer spending alone by Americans will account for $184 billion of that (see Figures 1.1 and 1.2). That's about the size of the entire economy of, say, Chile. That much retail spending will be a hefty hike from the $20 billion in retail shopping by Americans in 1999.

Table 1.1 Growth of Worldwide Internet Commerce

	2000	*2001*	*2002*	*2003*	*2004*	*Percent of Combined Offline/Online Sales in 2004*
Global Total (in billions of U.S. dollars)	$657.0	$1223.6	$2231.2	$39979.7	$6789.8	8.6%
North America	$509.3	$908.6	$1,495.2	$2,339.0	$3,456.4	12.8%
United States	$488.7	$864.1	$1,411.3	$2,817.2	$3,189.0	13.3%
Asia Pacific	$53.7	$117.2	$286.6	$724.2	$1,649.8	8.0%
Japan	$31.9	$64.4	$146.8	$363.6	$880.3	8.4%
Western Europe	$87.4	$194.8	$422.1	$853.3	$1,533.2	6.0%
Germany	$20.6	$46.4	$102.0	$211.1	$386.5	6.5%
Latin America	$3.6	$6.8	$13.7	$31.8	$81.8	2.4%
Rest of World	$3.2	$6.2	$13.5	$31.5	$68.6	2.4%

Global electronic commerce on the Internet will expand a stunning tenfold between 2000 and 2004. The bulk will occur in the United States. (Totals may not equal sum of rows due to rounding.)
Source: Forrester Research, Inc.

- ✔ In pursuit of those online dollars, Internet advertising will skyrocket to $33 billion by 2004. Of that, $22 billion will be spent pitching messages to eyeballs onscreen in the United States, up from a modest $2.8 billion spent in 1999. The 2004 total will exceed the money spent on advertising in magazines and yellow pages and on radio.
- ✔ Investors will have $3.1 trillion of their dollars invested through online accounts by 2004. That will be an eightfold increase over the amount of online investing in 1999.
- ✔ Contrary to the popular image, Net surfing is not an exclusively male pastime. Already, women are 41 percent of the Internet pop-

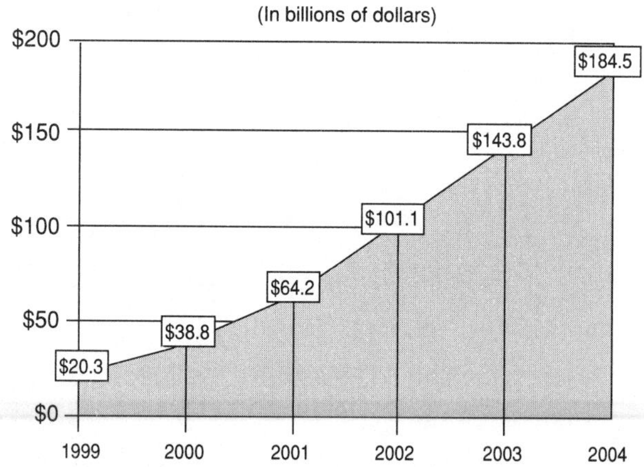

FIGURE 1.1 Total U.S. online retail revenues.
Consumer spending by Americans in the year 2000 accounts for $38.8 billion of the $657 billion in total worldwide electronic commerce on the Internet. Americans will shop 'til they drop even more in coming years—good news to electronic retailers and investors alike.
Source: Forrester Research, Inc.

> ulation, says the research firm Angus Reid Group. And by far more women than men—9 million versus 6.5 million—went online for the first time in the most recent six-month period, according to a head count by the Pew Internet & American Life Project.

That explains the prominence in online sales of goods and services aimed at women at least as much as men: clothing, flowers, housewares, home appliances, specialty gifts, health and beauty aids, groceries.

WHO'S ONLINE?

So people are swarming online. But exactly who are they? The largest single age group is young Baby Boomers—people 35 to 44 years old. As

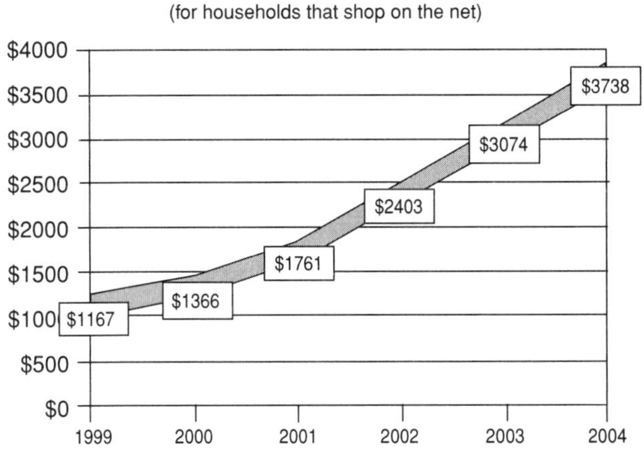

FIGURE 1.2 Average online spending.
As Americans become more comfortable shopping online—and as e-tailers improve cyber shopping opportunities—people will spend more money on the Internet. That will translate into fatter revenues and juicier profits for companies you can invest in.
Source: Forrester Research, Inc.

the pie chart in Figure 1.3 shows, they account for nearly 25 percent of Internet users, according to Media Metrix, a New York company that tracks demographics in cyberspace.

The second-largest online age group is young adults aged 25 to 34. These Gen-Xers, who were born after Baby Boomers, make up about 21 percent of Net users.

Older Baby Boomers and seniors—people 45 to 64 years old—are the third-largest slice of the population pie, at 20 percent.

Next in line are members of Generation Y, 18-to-24-year-olds, who account for more than 17 percent of the cyberpopulace. These are college and grad students, young military service members, and workers likely entering the labor force for the first time.

The balance of the Internet's population amounts to almost 17 percent, and is made up of people younger than 18 and older than 64.

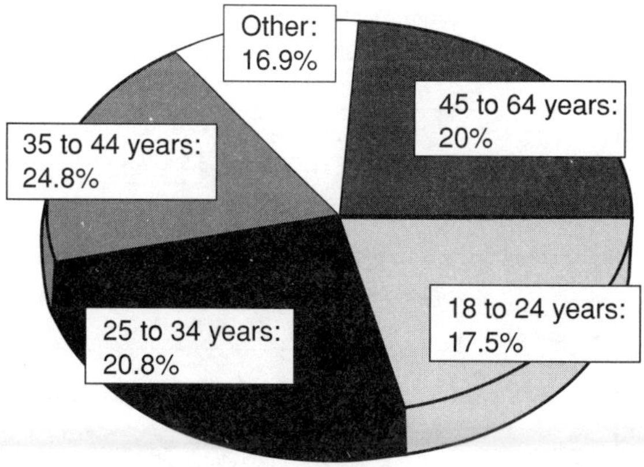

FIGURE 1.3 Internet users (by age groups).
By far, most people using the Internet are Baby Boomers and people approaching traditional retirement age. Those affluent age groups spend more time online than younger Web surfers, and they have lots of money to spend on big-ticket items from new cars to large screen TVs.
Source: Media Metrix.

The differences among various age segments of the Net's population are subtle, but they have dramatic consequences at the cash register:

1. Nearly two-thirds of Internet users are free-spending young adults or increasingly affluent Baby Boomers.
2. Boomers and seniors along with 18-to-24-year-olds are the most frequent newcomers to the cyberneighborhood.

What does that mean to you as an investor?

For one thing, it means good news. Those monied Boomers and seniors, says Media Metrix, "surf the Net more frequently, stay there longer, and check out more Internet pages than even their college-age counterparts." That, Media Metrix adds, debunks the myth that older Americans are technolaggards. This translates into revenues for lifestyle- and health-oriented web sites, says Doug McFarland, senior vice president of Media Metrix.

"Internet marketers with an eye on the future are discovering how focusing on this overlooked, high-spending audience can be a wise business strategy," McFarland reports on his firm's web site.

It gets better, Media Metrix says. These Boomers and seniors have disposable income, and they spend it. They're the age group most likely to own fax machines and copiers, large-screen TVs, and satellite dishes.

Nor is their spending limited to high-tech gadgets. They have the most credit cards and highest usage, they have the highest percentage of frequent-flier members, and they are more likely to buy a new car than a used one.

They also turn the stereotype of young adults as techno-addicts on its head. Compared with 18-to-24-year-olds, Boomers and seniors spend an average of 6.3 more days per month online, says McFarland's firm. They also stay logged on 235.7 minutes longer, and they view 178.7 more unique pages each month. As Baby Boomers might say, those are *far out* economic numbers, dudes.

And as Boomers and seniors grow more used to finding their way around the Web, they're likely to spend more time—and money—there, McFarland says. That's money in the bank if you are an advertiser looking for eyeballs, or if you are a retailer looking for customers, or if you are a business exec looking for colleagues in your industry, or if you are an *investor* in those kinds of online businesses.

ALL GOOD THINGS MUST PEAK

The Web's trend sounds perfect, doesn't it? Exploding numbers of extravagant big-spenders, fueling an economic boom without an end in sight.

The trouble is that the Internet's boom *will* have ups and downs. The enormous stock-market gains by Net businesses in the late 1990s, for example, were put into painful perspective by the abrupt setback that started in the spring of 2000.

The Net's popularity will also go through longer-term cycles, just like other aspects of human life. Take sports. In the 1920s and 1930s, baseball and boxing reigned supreme. Today, boxing still has lots of fans, but it is far from the audience magnet it used to be. Heck, even baseball has slipped behind such sports as auto racing in drawing spectators.

In the case of the Internet, its phenomenal growth will be impacted by fluctuations in the online population.

Online retail trade will be affected by the buying habits of each age group.

Its current explosive expansion will level off in 2004 as the Net runs out of newcomers, Forrester Research forecasts. But surging growth will return to the Net as today's teens and twentysomethings who make up Generation Y approach their peak earning years in 2010.

On the business-to-business (B2B) side of the Internet, the Net will flourish as businesses expand their online activities. As expansion levels off, so will new investment opportunities. This cycle will occur in one geographic region after another, Forrester predicts. The more economically advanced a region is, the sooner it will peak and then level off.

North America will go through it first, leveling off by 2003. Western Europe will follow, leveling off in 2004. Asia, Africa, and the Middle East will start what Forrester calls the hypergrowth cycle in 2002, leveling off by 2010. But the stronger economies of Asia will ramp up faster along the way. In between, Latin America and Eastern Europe will see their businesses start the cycle in 2004 and 2005, respectively.

In other words, growth will be carried like the baton in a relay race. One region after another will sprint forward. As an investor, it won't matter much which region is hot at any given time. All you need to do is invest in companies doing business where the action is.

SHOW ME THE MONEY

The most common activity on the Net is studying nineteenth-century Russian literature.

Okay, just kidding.

The thing people are most likely to go online for is e-mail. From an investment perspective, that's almost worse news than studying old Russian writers would be. At least fans of Leo Tolstoi and his literary comrades would probably buy a lot of very expensive caviar, Siberian sable, and spicey vodka.

The trouble with e-mail is that hardly anyone needs to pay for it. E-mail service, in fact, is often available for free. So don't bother looking for e-mail service providers in which you can invest.

E-mail, though, is crucial to many companies' plans for making money on the Net. That's because they use e-mail as a come-on, a loss leader, a freebie to lure customers in the front door. Once customers have signed on for free e-mail service, they become part of a potential advertising audience. They're also potential retail shoppers. Truth to tell, they are fish in the barrel. They are a potential customers for all of the pay-for-service features offered by that Internet portal providing free e-mail.

And people do spend money online.

With a cumulative price tag of $7.7 billion, Americans spent more on leisure travel than anything online in 1999. But they did spend freely on other retail merchandise and services, as shown in Table 1.2.

Merchants sold $3.17 billion worth of computers, TVs, and other consumer electronics. People shelled out $1.62 billion for clothes, shoes, and apparel accessories. Shoppers paid $1.24 billion for software and another $1.2 billion for books. Even flowers are nothing to sneeze at. People ordered $354 million worth of petals, pots, stems, and bouquets.

All of those totals are projected to grow dramatically through 2004. New industries will get in on the online action, helping to boost future consumer outlays.

For example, the auto industry did virtually no online retail business in 1999. But it sold cars, trucks, sport utility vehicles, motorcycles, and so on worth $400 million in 2000. Business is expected to grow nearly fivefold in 2001, and reach $16.6 billion by 2004. And that big-ticket figure doesn't include a penny of the $200 million in their own purchases of parts and materials that Detroit's Big Three automakers plan to steer through an online exchange.

Table 1.2 How We Spend Money Online	1999	2000	2002	2004
Total U.S. retail spending (in millions of dollars)	$20,252	$38,755	$101,128	$184,481
Media	3,617	5,461	10,091	12,598
Software	1,240	1,898	2,964	3,290
Books	1,202	1,715	2,724	3,279
Music	848	1,386	3,213	4,286
Videos	326	463	1,190	1,743
Event tickets	300	669	1,926	3,929
Apparel	1,620	3,607	14,710	27,128
General apparel	1,061	2,566	12,333	22,516
Footwear	121	290	605	1,085
Accessories	438	751	1,772	3,527
Gifts & flowers	656	998	2,853	4,659
Flowers	354	559	1,565	2,472
Greetings	134	177	587	798
Specialty gifts	167	271	701	1,389
Household goods	250	618	2,084	5,755
Recreation	595	2,139	6,961	15,039
Toys & video games	253	610	1,739	3,663
Sporting goods	165	586	1,949	4,220
Tools & garden	177	944	3,273	7,156
Leisure travel	7,798	13,950	26,042	32,097
Automobiles	—	400	4,500	16,567
Electronics	3,170	5,785	15,317	24,211
Computer hardware	1,964	3,471	9,154	12,541
Consumer electronics	1,205	2,315	6,163	11,670
Housewares	446	1,000	2,584	5,908
Appliances	179	405	756	2,023
Furniture	268	595	1,828	3,884
Food & beverage	513	1,132	5,009	16,863
Health & beauty	509	1,189	3,833	10,335
Miscellaneous	778	1,807	5,219	9,394

We already spend money online on a wide variety of retail goods and services. Spending will grow rapidly in coming years. Sellers of health-and-beauty aids are expected to make it significantly easier for their customers to shop online. And latecomers like the auto industry will dramatically add to the Internet's bottom line.

Source: Forrester Research, Inc.

The car industry is hardly alone in harnessing the Net for wholesale commerce. Paper, chemicals, large-scale real-estate owners, convenience-store suppliers, home-building suppliers, restaurant fish buyers, even consultants for dot-com firms . . . you name it, and mainstream industries are also jumping on the Internet bandwagon.

They see the Net as a place where they can force suppliers to compete head-to-head for business, leading to lower purchase costs on the ingredients they use. The speed of communication and the ability to centralize information will help them slash inventory delivery times.

It gets even better. Your investment choices are not restricted to just online retailers (often called B2C or *business-to-consumer* firms) or B2B enterprises. You can invest in companies that rarely or never set foot in cyberspace, but whose own revenues expand because they sell goods and services to businesses that *do* trade online.

Parcel-delivery services like to joke that they don't sell anything online and yet are the biggest beneficiaries of the Internet. But the FedExes of the world do help customers track deliveries by conducting online dragnets.

Finally, one of the largest and healthiest categories of Internet investments is made of companies that build the Net's skeleton. These are firms that make the Internet's infrastructure: the telephones, computers, and software, the microprocessor guts of so many high-tech gizmos, the underground cables, wireless transmission towers, and digital cameras—all of the things that must work behind the scenes so people can receive e-mail, send birthday cards, play online games, order computer monitors, listen to music, catch up on news, deposit a paycheck, and gossip about the hottest Internet stocks.

The investment opportunities are concentrated in the fields of technology and telecommunications. But they also span every sector of industry.

In Chapters 2 and 3 we'll explain how to tell one category of Internet business from another. And starting in Chapter 4 we'll discuss how to make investment decisions.

Chapter 2

How the Internet Works

What the heck is it about the Internet that so many people find so irresistible? Basically, it is the speed and convenience of a new form of communication.

The Net is an elaborate, nearly science-fiction improvement on the conventional phone call. It is a system that lets you send a book's worth of information with the ease of a phone call, all wrapped in a package with the entertainment value of television's moving images.

Soon, the technology will let people do things they can't do any other way. For instance, Senselt Technologies, an Israeli firm, is sniffing out ways to send scents over the Internet. The company wants to enable TVs, desktop computers, game consoles, and cellular phones to emit a wide bouquet of aromas. You could be watching a web-transmitted movie, for example, when the hero and heroine approach a rose bush. At that moment, a signal is sent to a device on or near your computer containing aromatic cartridges. The signal releases just the right mix of odors to produce the fragrance of roses in your multimedia entertainment room or office. When the aroma cartridges run dry after many uses, they could be replaced like the ink cartridges in a fax or computer printer.

But for the most part, the Internet's allure is that it helps people save time and money with familiar tasks at work and play.

BEAM ME UP, SCOTTY

The Internet is a form of catalogue shopping, flung forward at warp speed into the twenty-second century—only it is *now*. It is a process that lets people find things, research things, buy things, communicate something, pay something, play something—all in less time or at lower cost than it takes to do it the old-fashioned way.

In our modern age, drowning in stress, people don't have enough quality time for themselves, let alone for other people. Being able to do more in less time is increasingly valuable. Saving money, well, the virtue of *that* has never needed an explanation.

Online, people do the same things they do on Main Street or in the privacy of their homes—only more of it, or cheaper, or much faster, or more easily.

For example, you'd expect that only people confined to bed or a chair by illness or infirmity might spend much of their time at home reading their mail and penning letters to others. But sending or receiving e-mail is the most common reason people cite for going online. Ninety-three percent of people say that's why they go onto the Net, according to research firm Jupiter Research. Naturally, that includes people going online at work, sending or receiving business memos.

The second-most common online activity is use of a search engine to find something, such as a new article or a web site that a friend has recommended.

Studying something like new cars or a potential investment is the third-most-often-cited reason, at 78 percent. Selecting and sending greeting cards are other common reasons people log on. Scoping travel destinations and airline schedules are two more big draws. Even doing research for work is another popular reason for going online. Basically, the activities that draw people online most frequently are things that are easy to automate.

Using e-mail, looking up information, checking stock quotes, downloading software, booking travel arrangements—those are the sorts of things people most often go online to do.

Figure 2.1 shows the most popular online activities. Most of the activities are familiar. So far, few are mind-boggling in their novelty, but that doesn't matter. They add so *much* convenience and speed to ordinary tasks that they attract huge numbers of users. In turn, huge numbers of merchants follow, eager to accommodate. That makes the Internet into an *engine*, powering an enormous amount of new business activity.

No wonder Peter Drucker, a well-known business-management guru, has compared the Internet's importance to the steam engine.

"E-commerce," Drucker wrote in *The Atlantic Monthly*, "is to the Information Revolution what the railroad was to the Industrial Revolution—a totally new, totally unprecedented, totally unexpected development. And like the railroad 170 years ago, e-commerce is creating a new and distinct boom, rapidly changing the economy, society, and politics."

Fortunes were built in the nineteenth century thanks the railroad's ability to speed up the pace of trade, expand business opportunities, open new entrepreneurial frontiers, and lower the costs of doing business. Further, the railroad steam engine gave birth to industries and technologies that had nothing to do with steam or with steam engines.

The Internet is also expanding business, and it is leading to new technologies and new industries. And it too will make a widening circle of people wealthy.

ANATOMY OF A NEW TECHNOLOGY

If you venture on an elephant photo safari, it helps to be able to recognize a pachyderm. The same holds true if you're hunting for Internet profits. So here's what the critter is.

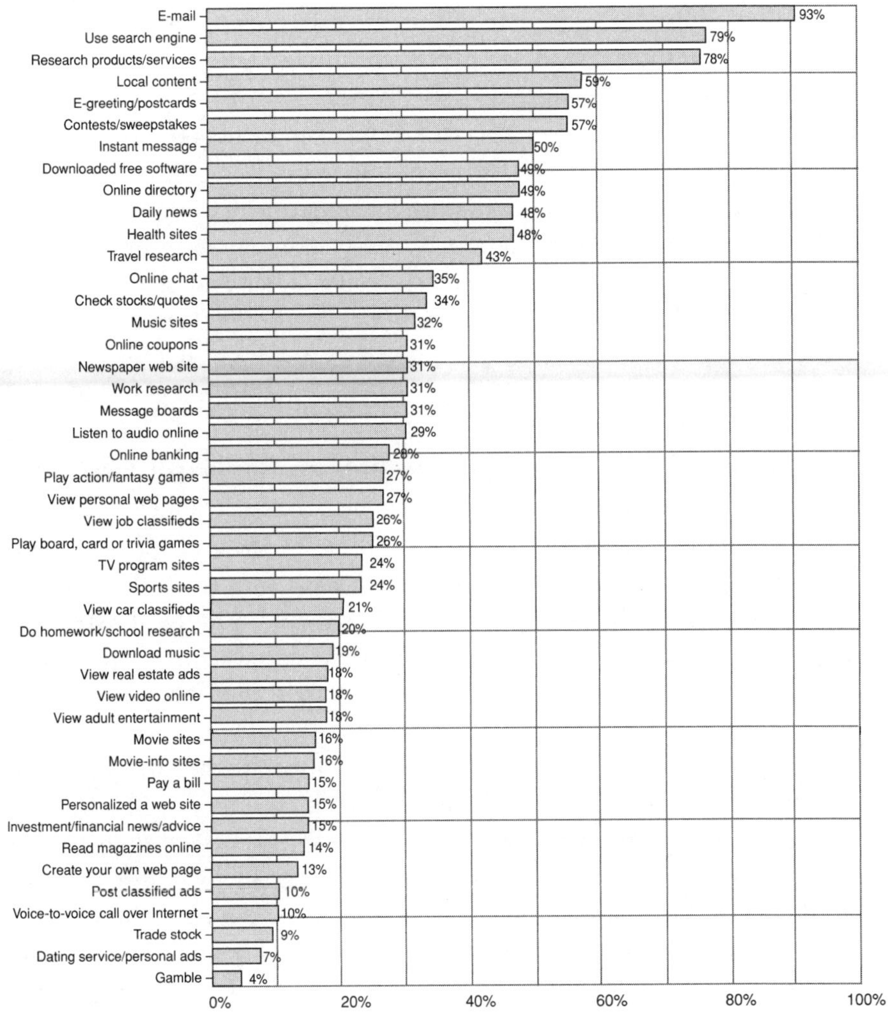

FIGURE 2.1 The most popular online activities.

People are more likely to go online for practical reasons than merely for entertainment. E-mail easily leads the list of tools that people want to use online, with 93 percent of Web surfers going online at least once a month for that purpose. Amusement and leisure-related sites are in the bottom half of motives for using the Net. Visiting a sports site, for instance, was cited by only 24 percent of users as the reason they go online.

Source: Jupiter Research.

The Internet is simply a large, global computer network. In fact, it is a network of networks.

Each network ties together computers, maybe only a few, maybe hundreds or thousands. They are connected so they can share information, giving each person access to more resources than any single computer is able to handle or to information that is compiled in remote, dispersed locations. Each of those smaller networks is called *an internet*. Working together, those internets are called *the Internet*.

It began in the late 1960s as a small network of computers used by the military. By 1970 this network had grown into something called the Advanced Research Projects Agency Network (ARPANET), and it was supported by the U.S. Defense Department. Nonmilitary users got in on the fun as universities and companies doing defense-related research were given access. During the 1980s the network opened to more universities and businesses.

Many people think the words *Internet* and *World Wide Web* refer to the same thing. They don't. The Internet consists of computers and computer programs, including the group of programs that make up the Web. The Web is one part of the larger Internet. The Internet is made up of the Web as well as non-Web software, plus all the computers that use those programs.

The World Wide Web was introduced in 1989. Developed by British computer scientist Timothy Berners-Lee, the Web consists of software programs and rules governing the way that text and pictures appear onscreen. Its programs also control video images and audio that run with the onscreen information.

The key feature to all of this is that the Internet and Web are run from outside your home or office computer. They are not operated by the software in your desktop or laptop PC. In fact, some Web entrepreneurs are betting they can convert a lot of people to use computers run by software *on* the Internet, not inside the PC. Even the applications software—the programs that run everything from word-processing to spreadsheets—would operate by remote control from the Net.

What You See Is What You Get

One big reason the Web is so popular is that it's relatively easy to use. Like most PCs these days, it's controlled through pictures onscreen. The system of onscreen picture commands is called a *graphical user interface* (GUI). Many readers of this book can remember the bad old days, when the only way they could control their computers was by typing lots of hard-to-remember commands. For years, there was no such thing as switching back and forth among various tasks on different screens. Unless you had an Apple, you didn't have onscreen buttons with images of commands and operations.

One big lure of the Web is that users can let the system update and improve its GUI. Ditto for letting the Web's countless providers of content fine-tune their products. Individual users don't have to bother with the cost and effort of buying updated versions of every software program they rely on.

And don't forget how hard it was in the old days (that is, a couple of years ago) to use different software programs on the same computer, let alone software from some *other* computer. Different generations of the same program often couldn't work together. Never mind how fruitless it commonly was to try copying, say, a table with accounting data from a Brand X spreadsheet into your Brand A word-processing program. They literally didn't speak the same language. Those roadblocks were multiplied when you tried to bring a copy of something, *anything*, from your computer onto someone else's.

On the Net, those problems are largely overcome. Big computers, using software programs whose bulging muscles could put Arnold Schwarzenegger to shame, do jobs that your pipsqueak software can't get a grip on.

The industrial-strength Net makes it possible, even handy, for you and millions of other people to use and coordinate far-flung resources. It is relatively easy for users to see and manipulate information from various sources on a series of online screens, switching back and forth from one to another. You rarely have to think about whether the underlying software is compatible with your own.

URL

Internet addresses are called URLs, for Uniform Resource Locator. A URL tells you how to reach a site on the Web. Some URLs are numbers, but because those can be hard to remember, other formats are used for identifying addresses.

Take the imaginary URL *http://www.sweetco.megacorp.com/candycane/sugarfree*. The *http* tells you that *hypertext transfer protocol* is the computer language you can use to get to this site. The address is the web site named for its *host*, the Sweet Co. division of the corporate conglomerate Mega Corp. The *com* after *megacorp* tells you that this is a commercial site. (A *gov* would mean it's a government-agency site. An educational institution site would use *edu*.) Within that site, the specific location is the *file* for sugar-free products, within the candy cane *directory*.

And, of course, it is the Web that gives us the ubiquitous *www* prefix for addresses on the Internet.

"In the Beginning . . ."

The reason all of this seems so new is that it wasn't until 1993 that commercial firms were allowed to sell access service to the Net to individuals. When that happened, network usage exploded.

It was as if Alexander Graham Bell had invented the telephone *after* phone lines already crisscrossed the nation on telephone poles and in underground tunnels. When individuals got access to the Internet in the early nineties, the basic infrastructure was up and running, ready for them.

People like you could start to send and receive e-mail. Soon, kids were playing computer games and businesses were swapping financial reports. It wasn't long before lingerie retailers began to broadcast fashion shows, featuring their scantily clad models. Financial services firms now peddle mutual funds. And wholesalers trade everything from apples to zirconium rings.

Two tools that let you use information online are *browsers* and *search engines*. Some people mistakenly use the terms interchangeably, as if they do the same jobs. But they're not the same.

Browser Software that lets you navigate the Internet. It enables you to see and hear things on the Web, such as text, graphics, sound, and video. Two popular examples are Netscape Navigator and Microsoft Internet Explorer.

Search engine This is a service that helps you *find* material online. You use one by typing in words or phrases, known as *keywords*. The tool then finds and lists web sites that contain the information you're seeking. Some fancy search engines have started to offer more services and content of their own, making themselves into *portals*.

Many people get onto the Internet through a computer that's part of a participating network, such as at their workplace or a research institution. But most casual users get onto the Net through a *portal*. Portals may provide free access or charge a fee. They also typically offer other attractions, such as e-mail, games, discussion groups, chat rooms, information resources such as encyclopedias, and investment news and research. Examples of portals are America Online (AOL) and Microsoft Network (MSN).

People reach a portal through an *Internet service provider* (ISP). Basically, ISPs have telecommunications and other equipment to link into the Internet.

THE BATTLE OVER BANDWIDTH

One of the Internet's most irritating limitations is slow transmission speed. This should not come as a surprise. After all, the Net was developed by the government, the same folks who gave us the Post Office and its best-known product, snail mail. Further, the Internet was designed to survive being nuked—presumably by the Commies, not some irate mail carrier who had gone postal.

So the Net can take a licking and keep on ticking. It just can't do it very quickly.

The amount of information a network can carry is measured in *bits* per second. A bit is the smallest piece of information that computers can process. Most network devices usually have the capacity—known as *bandwidth*—to carry thousands of bits (kilobits) or millions of bits (megabits) per second. If a network device has a capacity of, say, 64 kilobits, it is described as having a speed of 64Kbps (or "64K").

A network's overall transmission speed depends on the bandwidth of the slowest component along the way. The whole network's bandwidth can only be as fast as the smallest-capacity device that's used. In many cases, transmission speed also slows down as more people crowd onto a given network.

Bandwidth is what determines how quickly graphics form on your computer screen, or how quickly you can jump from one site to another on the Net. Naturally, individuals and businesses crave speed. Slow transmission is not only distracting and annoying, it also makes certain online products impractical or impossible. Fancy graphics or regular movies, for example, require high bandwidth. Fortunately, technology companies race each other to help Internet users rev up their engines. Businesses constantly bring higher-bandwidth devices to market at ever-lower prices.

Increasing bandwidth is a never-ending theme of Internet competition. Even once a company is plugged into the Internet, it searches for faster and faster access. That's why successive generations of devices and transmission lines replace older ones. And growing numbers of companies try to bring their own next-generation hardware to market before their competition does.

Investors who put their money in companies that do the best jobs of selling wider bandwidth can make a killing.

Chapter 3

Internet Sectors

In the previous chapter, we compared an elephant safari to hunting for profits in Internet investments. Well, not only is an elephant a good metaphor for Internet investments, but understanding the Net can be as confusing as recognizing an elephant was to the four blind men of the famous old fable.

You remember the story. Four blind men approached a baby elephant. One blind man found the elephant's tail, and decided the whole animal must be like a length of rope. Another blind man touched the beast's leg, and he was sure the creature resembled a tree trunk. When the third blind man grabbed the pachyderm's trunk, it reminded him of an anaconda, the fattest of snakes. And the fourth blind man thought the elephant was a wall when he touched its firm, broad side.

The point is that Internet investments are as varied as the many parts of an elephant. In fact, Internet investments fit into five broad categories. Understanding them will show you how Wall Street thinks about the Internet. That's important because Wall Street doesn't like to compare apples and oranges. An investment decision is often based on how fast and how reliably a company's profits are expected to grow. And companies in different circumstances can have very different prospects for future profits.

So Wall Street professionals start *their* Internet investment decisions by comparing how companies within each category stack up against each other. You can do the same thing. We'll start by getting a handle on what types of companies fit into each category, and how the categories differ from each other.

The categories are:

- ✔ Portals
- ✔ Content
- ✔ E-commerce
- ✔ Infrastructure
- ✔ Venture capital

WEB PORTALS

A portal is where most people enter the Internet. America Online is the biggest and best-known commercial portal. Others include Yahoo! and Lycos.

But if the Internet is a humongous cyberspace carnival, jam-packed with attractions, then portals are more than just the entrance. They're the carny barkers themselves. They urge people to check out the action, and they show people the way in. And there's quite a lot going on inside this Big Top. In fact, the number of individual web sites leaped from about 3.3 million in 1999 to 5 million in 2000, according to "The Standard," an online news periodical that reports on the Internet.

The Web's sites cover every topic you can imagine, and then some. Aardvarks? There are hundreds of web sites with that word in their title; some sites are actually devoted to the animal itself. Zygote? Not as popular as aardvarks, but there are still dozens of web sites named for the cell that's formed by the union of a human sperm and a human egg.

Some portals also offer services of their own (or provided by third-party subcontractors) such as search engines, e-mail, information resources, access to online brokerages, and chat groups (discussion forums). Portals generally charge subscribers for Internet access on a monthly or yearly basis. A growing number offer free service.

Both fee-for-access and free-service portals typically want as many visitors as possible. The heavier the traffic, the more they can charge e-businesses for prominent "storefronts"within the portal "mall." Also, they can charge advertisers higher rates. Portals providing free service commonly bombard users with more advertisements or ads that are more prominent (and distracting, if not downright annoying) onscreen.

CONTENT

This category consists of information and entertainment material that draws people online. It includes news, games, music, and research information.

A lot of it is copyrighted material provided by well-known companies. For example, many newspapers provide their reports to one or more portals' subscribers. It may be the same or a revised version of articles that appear in the print versions of the publications. Some portals feature those news stories as a special service of the portal itself. Sometimes you get access to the articles only by going through the portal to the publication's own web site.

When a portal offers articles as a feature, subscribers generally get those articles for free—at least when they are initially presented. If you go to a publication's own web site, you may have to pay an additional subscription fee for access to articles.

Portals rely on content to lure visitors. As the Internet grows, demand for fresh and attractive content is growing an estimated 20 percent to 25 percent annually, according to WWW Internet Fund.

E-COMMERCE

Electronic commerce involves selling merchandise or service using the Internet. When one business sells to another business, it's known as business-to-business (B2B) e-commerce. When the customer is a consumer, it's referred to as business-to-consumer (B2C) e-commerce. These subcategories are similar to the distinctions between wholesale and retail in the non-Internet, or bricks-and-mortar, world.

E-commerce transactions involve all sorts of goods and services, from books and CDs to airline tickets, hotel reservations, computer hardware, peripherals, and software.

Consumers like e-commerce because of its novelty, convenience, and low costs. You may not be able to kick a car's tires online, but you can see color pictures of more models than any one dealer could hope to stock. You can also read reviews, study vehicle specifications, compare features, and custom-mix options to your heart's content. All from the comfort of your den (or, if your boss doesn't mind or doesn't notice, from your office).

Businesses love e-commerce because it can increase revenues. It does that by providing a new place to sell goods and services. It boosts revenues as surely as adding stores to a retail chain, expanding the size of existing stores, or hiring additional wholesale account reps. Only it costs a fraction of what those cost. Building a web site is a bargain compared with building, buying, leasing, or remodeling storefronts. A web site doesn't have as much built-in overhead for security guards and heat at night when the building is almost devoid of human life. And you don't have to pay as much health insurance and other benefits for people running a web site. In fact, by providing an alternative way to do business that lowers costs, e-commerce can improve a company's bottom line even if the the top line, revenues, doesn't increase.

Better yet, e-commerce makes other cost savings possible too. It can reduce inventory, shorten product life cycles, speed up customer service, and turbocharge distribution. In fact, by linking those tasks with computerized accounting systems, it can stretch a company's working capital. It also lowers the cost of each of those tasks individually.

The Net provides that computerized method for splicing together corporate functions. It smooths out or eliminates the bottlenecks between departments. It lets different parts of a business perform as efficiently together as they do individually. It makes a harmonious orchestra out of a bunch of soloists.

So why hasn't every e-commerce business flourished more? First of all, because the real world doesn't work as smoothly as most business plans cheerfully predict. One of the biggest differences is that online businesses don't escape all of the costs of brick-and-mortar stores after all. Online businesses may not need expensive storefronts, but they've discovered that they do need to build or rent warehouses filled with forklifts, conveyor belts, stocking clerks, and—yes—security guards at night.

Second, there aren't enough customers to keep every new cyberentrepreneur running at a profit.

So the efficiencies and cost-savings of e-commerce exist. But they won't bestow the Midas touch on every online merchant wannabe. Only the fittest will survive and prosper. Some will be outright business newcomers, with no offline operations. Many will be bricks-and-clicks enterprises, companies expanding already existing offline businesses into the brave new realm of opportunities provided by the Internet.

INFRASTRUCTURE

If the Internet is an Information Superhighway, then all of that highway's roads, traffic signals, toll booths, directional signs, on and off ramps, and roadside rest areas are its infrastructure.

Those physical things include everything from the cables and wires that carry electricity and pulses of light to all of the gizmos they're connected to or that they transmit to. It includes things as large as those roadside towers that catch and relay signals from cell phones and wireless laptop computers, which don't need to be plugged into a phone jack. It includes the tiny microchips that are the brains inside everything from—well, virtually *everything*.

Moreover, companies that make or supply the Internet's infrastructure often fare better than dot-com companies. Look what happened in early 2000, when the market slumped, which it does from time to time. By one low point on May 23, the overall market had fallen 11.3 percent from its high point. The Internet sector drooped even more. A key reason was that everyone and his uncle was starting Internet businesses. The number grew into a tidal wave that overwhelmed Wall Street's ability to spoon-feed them with operating cash. As Net companies started to go hungry, Wall Street panicked at the idea that some might starve to death. Stock prices fell.

But investors did not abandon all parts of the Internet equally. They heavily sold off stocks of companies that sell goods and services to consumers online. After all, how many dozen stores peddling pet food online can the Internet support?

Yet construction of the Information Superhighway didn't slow as quickly or as sharply. Phone companies kept laying cable. Semiconductor companies kept squeezing more memory onto computer chips. So investors held tight to much of their stock in companies building the Net.

Look at two mutual funds run by Kinetics Asset Management, which specializes in Internet investments. During one bad nine-week stretch, Kinetics Internet Infrastructure Fund (which invests only in Internet infrastructure companies) lost nearly 39 percent in value. Bad as it was, that was better than its stablemate's performance. Kinetics Internet Emerging Growth Fund, which invests in small dot-coms, many of which are such raw newcomers to business that they have scant or zero profits, lost nearly 53 percent.

Bob Kippes, Internet-savvy lead manager of AIM Aggressive Growth Fund, told *Investor's Business Daily* how he minimized damage to his $4.5 billion fund during that market downturn, despite being loaded with Internet stocks: "[S]tocks with little or no earnings [got] shelled [during the market decline]. A lot of Internet names, with no earnings, they're all smoke and mirrors. . . . We believe you can play infrastructure, the building of the Internet, as opposed to pure Net plays. And that's saved us. . . ."

Kippes wasn't alone. Many professional investors who wanted to continue owning stock in Internet companies cut their risk by focusing on infrastructure businesses.

Companies helping to *build* the Internet fared far better than businesses that peddle goods and services *on* the Internet. Their relative good fortune was reminiscent of Levi Strauss's success, which we described in Chapter 1. Selling jeans to miners during the Gold Rush, he was an infrastructure entrepreneur of his day.

Routers

One of the key gizmos in this zoo of exotic electronic critters is called a *router*. As we explained in Chapter 1, while computers called *servers* store information and software programs and dish them out to people using other computers, a router is a special computer devoted to directing or routing data over networks. It's the traffic cop of the Information Superhighway. Its role is so important—and so many routers are used by the Internet's nearly countless networks—that the leading manufacturer of routers, Cisco Systems, Inc., emerged as the single best-performing stock of the 1990s.

A router chooses a path across a network for the data it handles. Its job is to make sure data gets from one network to another. To do its work, a router must deal with enormous volumes of information. Cisco's fastest router as of December 1999, for example, could process about 16 million requests for web pages a second.

As Internet use explodes, to compete for business manufacturers will have to make routers that not only can handle more data but can do it more quickly. And demand for routers themselves will also expand dramatically. In 1999 alone, some $2 billion was spent on high-speed routers, the backbone of major data networks, according to *Investor's Business Daily*. By 2003, that figure will jump to $16 billion. And that's just one category of router.

Networking

One slice of the infrastructure pie is networking. This category includes the hardware and software companies that manufacture the routers and other gizmos called *switches* and *hubs*, which keep everything flowing smoothly through the Internet. As these devices are forced to become increasingly sophisticated so they can carry more video and sound as well as voice and data, they will evolve into higher versions of themselves. Like creatures in some Darwinian jungle, fighting for survival in the marketplace, some will eventually give rise to new products, entirely new circuit-bearing species. From their sales, new business fortunes will be made.

Software

In its broadest sense, the infrastructure pie also includes the various software programs that tell the Internet's computers what to do. This infrastructure category is very wide and diverse. It has separate subsectors for software that takes care of security (performing tasks such as making sure some stranger isn't stealing your credit-card numbers from online merchants) and for software that runs things like search engines, e-mail, and banking operations. This category is sometimes called *tools*.

Wireless

Another major category concerns *wireless* communications. Until recently, the only personal exposure most people had to the wireless revolution was when *another* person disturbed everyone around them by using a cell phone in a restaurant or movie theater. But increasing numbers of people are finally getting their own cell phone, personal digital assistant, or beeper as technical advances make it easier, faster, and cheaper to send *data* whizzing to and from handheld devices.

Wireless no longer is a tool affordable only by yuppie bankers and drug dealers working their local street corner. More and more people are buying cell phones and a dizzying array of voiceless handheld appliances. On their compact display panels, the devices show users data, names, and numbers they need for fun, business, and personal profit—everything from stock quotes to their business schedules, phone numbers, and brokerage account balances. In fact, some brokerages occasionally give free or discounted handheld devices to customers who sign up for new brokerage services.

The wireless devices are the visible tip of a technological iceberg, making more information instantly available to people. Behind the scenes, software is linking more databases storing information like stock prices. Hardware is part of the story too. Bigger and better routers, for example, relay information to customers faster.

Want a heads-up when your favorite stock reaches a price where it's worth selling it? Want to tell your brokerage at what price you'll buy some stock you've been tracking? Today you can get that alert or arrange that transaction when you want, no matter where you are.

That's the crux of the surging popularity of wireless: granting people mobility and convenience.

Wireless devices let you buy and sell stocks, receive and send information, anywhere. You don't have to wait until you're in your office or at home, where you can plug into a phone jack or high-speed cable. You can do it *now*, from the beach, from your car stuck in traffic, from your lover's hideaway, from your business meeting during an intermission.

Semiconductors

The growth of wireless telecommunications helps enlarge the market for computer chips, the brains behind all of the smart devices populating the world. This means more business for the makers of semiconductors, as well as for companies that make equipment used to manufacture various types of chips and to test the equipment and the chips themselves.

Storage Area Networks

The life blood of the Internet is information, data in countless forms. Servers dish it up, routers send it on its way. But before it goes anywhere, it resides in groups or networks of computers that specialize in storing it. Storage Area Networks (SANs) are responsible for stockpiling the Internet's ever-growing reservoirs of data.

Like a well-run warehouse for, say, furniture, a storage network not only must have large capacity. It also must be well organized so merchandise can be found, moved to a loading bay without being delayed by other furniture that's coming or going, and shipped, all as fast as possible.

The more efficiently a storage network works, the better. The best ones do their job without interfering with servers, routers, and other network utensils that transfer their data. After all, if you run a furniture company, you don't want salespeople from the showroom or bookkeepers from the accounting department to have to help speed things up in the warehouse. Then they are not able to do their *own* jobs.

Local Area Network (LAN) Don't confuse a LAN with a SAN. A LAN is simply a group of computers linked in a network. The computers generally are located near each other, as in a business office. Connecting them lets people on that network all have access to common sources of information, such as a company's sales records or accounting system.

Virtual Private Networks

Private businesses set up their own networks—virtually mini–America Onlines—to reduce costs and to improve privacy and security. These virtual private networks (VPNs) utilize the same lineup of software, servers, routers, and other equipment used by other networks that make up the Internet.

And as the Net itself grows worldwide, so will the use of VPNs and the revenue of companies selling hardware and software to build VPNs. WWW Internet Fund forecasts that VPNs will grow 40 percent to 50 percent annually through 2007.

VENTURE CAPITAL

While portals like America Online and e-commerce companies like Amazon.com are familiar to many people, venture capital firms are the phantoms of the Internet opera. But they perform a vital function. And they can make money.

Like full-grown eagles raising a nestful of eaglets, Internet venture capital firms provide money and other necessities of corporate life to fledgling Internet companies. They are investment firms that focus on the Internet. Typically, they take a hands-on approach, helping their progeny in a variety of ways. They recruit executives for the young companies. They help up-and-(hopefully)-coming companies find new customers and strategic partners by introducing them to one another. They encourage Net novices to share ideas and develop new products, services, and technologies. They advise them in matters ranging from marketing to shopping for office space.

Sometimes, investment firms provide young companies with a place to do business, where they share space with or are close neighbors to other young companies. An arrangement like that is called an *incubator*. It can help young companies cut expenses by sharing clerical costs, security, and so on. It can also make it easier for managers to interact and brainstorm together.

Investment firms often specialize in various niches of the Net. And some engage in other lines of business, such as online advertising or software services. Some Internet investment firms are CMGI, Softbank Corp., Internet Capital Group, and Wit Capital Group.

Overall, a venture capital firm's goal is to help young companies to grow. That makes the venture capital firm's investment in them more valuable. That's precisely what is achieved if the young company grows enough to become a publicly traded company. The rite of passage is the company's *initial public offering* (IPO) of stock.

By investing in an Internet venture capital firm, then, you get to invest in young companies working toward their own IPO. This gives you a chance to reap the potentially huge financial rewards of being in on the ground floor of a business whose stock skyrockets in value as the business grows and matures through various stages of corporate life.

But it also exposes you to the potential risks. When the company prunes the ranks of Internet firms, killing off many of the young and frail ones, venture capitalists are left holding a lot of worthless stock certificates. In turn, their own stock suffers. That's exactly what happened to them during 2000.

And risk is the norm on Wall Street. It is a perilous sea, which you wouldn't think of undertaking to cross without navigational tools. And that's this book's role. It is a navigational tool, to help you cut risks, max out potential gains, and stay afloat as you venture into a merciless ocean that can swallow sailors who set forth unprepared.

Chapter 4

First Steps with Internet Investments

If Wall Street is a perilous sea, the Internet is like Mt. Everest. To the unprepared climber, it seems unscalable.

Its technology is complex. How it works can seem baffling. It consists of many sectors, each different from another, each presenting new puzzles. And many of the Internet's businesses are so young and so lacking in earnings that it's hard to do the sort of normal financial analysis that would shed light on their chances for success. Their future prospects are as shrouded in mystery as the chronically fog-bound peak of Everest. But that's only for people who are unprepared.

Readers of *Getting Started in Internet Investing* are equipped to continue their ascent. You've learned the basics of what the Internet is and how it works. You know enough to climb the next step in learning to make Internet investment decisions. After all, you don't have to know how to assemble a computer to be able to use one. And you don't need a Ph.D. in electrical engineering to decide whether to invest in Dell Computer or People's Computer and Ox Cart Manufacturing Collective No. 13.

The fact is, knowing how to select Internet investments is a commonsense process. It consists of straightforward, logical steps. Once you strip away the Wall Street jargon and hocus-pocus, there is no mystery.

That process begins with three basic choices. You must decide:

1. How much can you afford to invest, whether it is in the Internet or any other industry?
2. Should you invest in the Internet in particular?
3. If so, how much?

A PRIMER ON INVESTING

The way to answer those questions is by asking them the right way: in the context of your overall finances.

The first question is a straightforward budget issue. Do you have disposable income left over after paying your living expenses?

The second and third questions are more complex than they may seem at first.

That's because of how much Internet stocks and mutual funds pitch up and down in price and value, especially in the short run. All shares of stocks and mutual funds rise and fall, but Internet shares can take you on a particularly wild rollercoaster ride over short spans of time.

Many Internet companies are young but they already face a lot of competition, which in many cases is growing and getting fiercer. Often, Internet firms lack the stability and predictability of large, well-established companies. Their revenues can fluctuate enough to make you seasick. They may still be struggling toward profitability. Many will fold and go out of business. So you've got to decide how much of your money to risk investing in these businesses.

That depends on a number of factors, such as which segments of the Internet you invest in and how much stock-market volatility you can stand. At what point do the market's sometimes feverish lurches up and down prevent you from sleeping at night?

Your decision can also depend on whether you buy shares of stock or mutual funds. Lots of factors can influence this decision, so we'll deal with it here and in more detail in Chapters 5 and 6. For now, let's focus on the simple budget question: Can you afford to invest?

The simple answer is that it depends on how much money you have. But there's more to it. How much money you have really means how much *of* your money is available for investments in general and Internet investments in particular. That depends on your income, living expenses, spending priorities and goals, age, and lifestyle.

Are you paying a mortgage? Probably. If you're a renter, your monthly nut isn't likely to be any smaller. Got children? If so, you know how expensive it can be just to raise them, let alone pay their way through Harvard and then medical school. Helping your elderly mother pay her living expenses? It's the least you can do for the person who changed your diapers, wiped your nose when you skinned you knee at the playground, *and* nursed you through a case of the measles.

Everyone's finances are different. If you own a yacht and make investment decisions in between port calls in the Mediterranean, the factors that influence your Internet investment decisions will be very different from the guy or gal trying to figure out whether he or she can afford a new Chevy this year. Heck, the factors you weigh won't even be identical to those considered by your fellow millionaire on the yacht berthed next to yours in Portofino.

Every investor's needs, objectives, and circumstances are unique. Even when others have the same goals you do, no one else has your precise mix of goals and means for reaching them. You and the fellow next door may both want the same expensive, new set of golf clubs. But he's 10 years older than you, has twice as many children, and a retirement nest egg one-third smaller than yours. The cost of those golf clubs, and of everything else in your lives, will impact your respective finances quite differently.

As a result, how each of you invests probably also will be quite different. Your investments will be designed to do different things.

For starters, the right mix depends on two things:

1. Your investment goals
2. Your investment time horizon

That's it. Those factors are the key to forming your Internet investment game plan. In fact, they are the key to forming your overall investment game plan, and for deciding how your Internet investments fit into that.

Once you have addressed those factors one at a time, like steps in a process, you will be ready for the fun part—selecting your investments!

CHOOSING YOUR INVESTMENT GOALS

The first step is to decide what your investment goals are. Translation: Decide what your *spending* goals are. How much you can invest—or whether you should invest in it at all—depends on how much of your money you need for other expenditures.

Sure, you want those new golf clubs, your spouse wants a new car, you both want the vacation home on Martha's Vineyard. The good news is, you can have it all. That is, if you live to be 200 years old. And your investment portfolio continues to grow, along with your bank account and your salary.

Otherwise, you'll have to make choices. This comes down to

> **Portfolio** All of your individual investments—whether they are stocks, bonds, mutual funds, or some other security—as a group. For example, if you are a member of a 401(k) plan, all of the investments in your account are your portfolio in the plan.

forming a budget and timetable. How much are you planning to spend for those golf clubs anyway? How about that car? The cottage on the Vineyard?

Likewise, which things do you want most? Which do you want first? Do you need some sooner than others? If one of your goals is, say, to pay for a daughter's wedding, the birds and the bees may have more say over the timing than your own idea of a logical agenda.

Start by making a list of your spending goals. Use the worksheet in Table 4.1. In fact, you may want to make photocopies of the worksheet so you can do new calculations for different years. This will give you an idea of how much of your current and future money is earmarked for specific spending goals, and how much you'll have left over for investing.

It will also help clarify the timing of upcoming expenditures. You might be able to help pay for anything more than two years away with the fruits of your investments in stock and stock mutual funds. That's because they grow in value over time. For that reason, they're generally known as *growth* investments. Money you initially invest ends up worth more. But along the way stocks and stock funds can also fall in value. Two years is the minimum amount of time you should allow for any stock or stock fund investment to bounce back and at least equal the money you started with.

If you plan to pay for something sooner than that, do it with money taken from certain types of conservative investments, savings, and ongoing income. These conservative investments include money market funds, bonds, and bond mutual funds, which don't gyrate much in value in short periods of time. The amount you set aside for, say, a down payment on a home will still be worth the same when closing day arrives.

The trade-off is that these investments don't grow much over time. They do provide income and short-term stability, though. They're known as *income* or *fixed-income* investments. Money market funds are sometimes called *cash equivalents*.

Table 4.1 Spending Goals Worksheet

Item/Goal	*Cost*	*Rank (if time & money were no object)*	*Deadline (date/ rank)*	*Order of Preference (in the real world, where time and money do matter!)*
Special & One-Time Expenditures				
	$			
Annual Living Expenses				
	$			
Total:				

Get a handle on how much money you expect to spend now and in the future. You should also organize your spending goals according to their importance.

PRIORITIZE

The next step is to prioritize your spending goals. Separate the mandatory expenses from optional expenses.

Do that by putting all of your routine expenses (like groceries, mortgage payments, health insurance) into one category called "Annual Living Expenses." List special and onetime expenditures separately. This is where to put next year's trip to Mardi Gras.

Don't forget to include contributions to your retirement accounts as part of your routine expenses.

In the third column, rank expenditures according to your priorities. Label the most important priority as Number 1, the next as Number 2, and so on.

Then, in the fourth column, rank them according to time horizon. Jot down the date by which you need to reach this goal, then rank the one you need first as Number 1 and continue in descending order (that is, the goal that can wait until last gets ranked with the biggest number).

Now see how closely your priorities and your time horizon match. In the fifth column, assigned a final order-of-preference number; this is the order in which you will actually tackle these goals. Some of your goals may have very different ranks in priority and time horizon. For those, you'll simply have to make a subjective decision about where in your personal pecking order it should stand.

REALITY CHECK

Now, let's see if you can you afford your goals. You'll find out by comparing your planned yearly expenditures with the money you expect to have available.

In the "Planned Expenditures" section of Table 4.2, write your total planned spending for this year and each year in question in one of the annual spending columns. Use totals from Table 4.1. Then see how it stacks up against your projected resources for that year.

Table 4.2 Investment Time-Horizon Worksheet

	2000	*2001*	*2002*	*2003*	*Year:____*	*Year:____*
Income						
Your salary						
Spouse's salary						
Other income (such as non-retirement savings and investments)						
Your pension						
Spouse's pension						
Social Security						
Your retirement accounts (such as 401(k) or IRA)						
Your spouse's retirement accounts (such as 401(k) or IRA)						
Total (line A):						
Planned Expenditures						
Total (line B):						
Subtract line B from line A:						

Subtract your planned expenditures (from Table 4.1) from each year's financial resources to see if you'll have money left over for investing. If line A is greater than line B, you've got enough money for investing.

To calculate your resources, add your sources of income: salary, spouse's salary, one or both pensions (if any), Social Security. To get a ballpark estimate of income from your retirement nest egg in any year, count on receiving 5 percent of it. Ditto for your spouse's, if he or she will be retired.

To see if your projected resources are larger than you planned expenditures, subtract line B from line A.

If your projected resources are larger, the difference is the amount you can invest.

If your spending will exceed your resources, you've either got to get a better-paying job or better returns on your investments—or you've got to cut back your planned expenditures. Eliminate the lowest priority ones first.

You don't need a lot of spare cash to get started. With as little as $25 a week, you can set aside enough to purchase shares of stock or mutual funds.

Now all you've got to do is decide what to invest in.

Chapter 5

Weighing Investment Risk

In Chapter 4 we posed three key questions:

1. How much can you afford to invest, no matter where—in the Internet or any other industry?
2. Should you invest in the Internet in particular?
3. If so, how much?

We have already answered the first of those questions via the worksheets in Chapter 4. You now know how much money you have available for investment.

The answer to the second question is Yes, depending on two things: if you want to invest in a vigorously growing new industry; and if you want to invest in companies best positioned to profit from that growth.

That makes it sound like a no-brainer. Who wouldn't want those benefits? But deciding what portion of your investment money to put into the Internet is anything but a no-brainer.

HOW MUCH SHOULD YOU INVEST IN THE INTERNET?

There are four good reasons why Internet stocks aren't the only thing everyone invests in.

First, there are top-performing stocks in other industrial sectors.

Second, not all Internet stocks do well.

Third, even high-flying Internet stocks can run out of gas; some refuel and take off again, some crash and burn.

Fourth, not all investors are comfortable with Internet stocks. For one thing, many gyrate wildly in price over short periods of time. As we described in the previous chapter, many Internet companies are young, face stiff competition, and lack the revenue and profits that give stability to many older, well-established corporations.

Those four factors fuel investor uncertainty. If you don't know how to objectively analyze a stock's prospects for price growth, it's not hard to be afraid you'll make some wrong investment selections. It's easy to be afraid that other investors have more reliable information. It's easy to be afraid of losing your shirt.

So emotion enters the equation for many investors, even though it shouldn't. Investors should be guided by facts and figures. They should invest in stocks best poised for big upward moves in their share prices. As investment mentor William J. O'Neil has explained, when it comes to individual stocks, that's determined by such factors as the strength, quality, and soundness of a business and its products or services. It's also determined by how a stock is performing in the marketplace.

So long as Internet stocks meet those standards, you should invest in them.

In fact, deciding what portion of your resources to invest in the Internet can be answered objectively. It's whichever stocks—Internet or otherwise—are best positioned for explosive growth at the time you're ready to invest.

But not all investors are ready to put their faith in objective analysis and invest their money on its results. Unfortunately, fear and uncertainty play a role for many investors.

In later chapters we will explain how you can rely on objective analysis rather than emotion. You should also consider reading *24 Essential Lessons for Investment Success* (New York: McGraw-Hill, 2000), a book about investment strategy written by Bill O'Neil, who is publisher of *Investor's Business Daily*.

In the meantime, to help readers who can't help but invest with their hearts as well as their smarts, we'll talk about how to assess your fear that your investments could explode on you. And we'll explain how to use that in deciding how much of your hard-earned investment money to put to work in Internet companies.

HOW MUCH RISK IS TOO MUCH?

Imagine this hypothetical scenario:

This morning the Federal Reserve (the Fed), the nation's central bank, announced a slight uptick in the rates it will charge big banks to borrow money. The result—a bewildering blizzard of seemingly contradictory reactions among Wall Street wizards:

- ✔ Stock prices of big commercial banks fell because the price of the chief raw resource they in turn sell to customers—money—has gone up.
- ✔ Supermarket stocks rose because people still have to eat.
- ✔ Car-makers' stocks plunged because these companies and their suppliers borrow so much money from commercial banks.
- ✔ Prices of existing 30-year government bonds fell because suddenly fewer people want to continue owning them. Why? Their *yield* (the interest they pay) is less than what will be paid by new bonds, whose rates will be higher, reflecting the higher cost of money set by the all-powerful Fed.

Businesses in different industries would not be the only ones with diverse responses to the Fed's fiscal news. As an investor, you are more comfortable with some new developments than others. You may not own stocks or bonds from, or mutual funds investing in, companies that are most impacted. Or you may have enough time to bounce back from whatever does affect them.

Basically, conditions in the world—whether they stem from political shenanigans, economic developments, or the whims of the marketplace—create more risk for some companies and investors, and less for others.

What knocks *you* for a financial loop may not faze the next guy or gal one whit. The investments you select will depend on what kinds of risk—and how much—you can handle. That requires you to determine your level of *risk tolerance*.

> **Risk tolerance** The amount of danger or volatility you can tolerate in your investments. It will vary according to such variables as your circumstances, age, income, financial resources, and amount of time before you need to use your money.

TYPES OF RISK

The best way to start is by understanding the different types of risk confronting any investor. Basically, there are four kinds:

1. Business risk
2. Interest risk
3. Market risk
4. Inflation risk

If you can predict the four kinds of risk reliably, you'll end up richer than Bill Gates. If you're like most individual investors, though, you usually learn about risk as you read about it in your morning newspaper—the day after it has struck. Either way, it pays to understand the differences among various sorts of investment peril:

Business risk. This is the most familiar risk. If a business is in danger of folding or running less profitably, it is a bad risk. Everyone understands that. But what about harder-to-recognize threats to a business's prospects? If you had worked for a buggy-whip maker in the year 1905 and you had just seen your first automobile drive by, would you have recognized the menace to your company's future? If you were a banker, would you have been willing to lend *your* money to the maker of a smoke-belching car? A company's success depends on the quality of its management, work force, products or services, finances, and marketing—all in comparison to its competition's.

Interest risk. Interest is the price of money, and it can rise and fall. Banks charge interest for loans. *You* charge your bank when you get a certificate of deposit. The rate at which you're willing to do that is the price you charge the bank to borrow your money. It all depends on how many people are competing for how few dollars. When interest rates change, they drag the value of certain investments up or down. After all, who wants a bond that pays 6 percent when you can get one for 8 percent? The interest rate remains fixed, but the price of that older bond must fall on the resale market; otherwise, no one would buy it. The risk? Getting stuck with lower-paying investments while interest rates are rising.

Market risk. The most handsome screen idol in Hollywood can be hit by a bus while crossing the street. There go the good looks. Likewise, any company can be blindsided by negative news. Let's say a Middle Eastern authoritarian regime unexpectedly invades a neighboring oil potentate. War erupts. Back home, your own company's customers hold back on spending because they're suddenly nervous about fuel supplies. Your revenues dwindle. Banks grow skittish about lending you money. Merchandise starts arriving late from your cash-starved suppliers. Your profits plummet, and the company's stock slides. As an investor, can you weather it?

Inflation risk. Inflation erodes the value of money. It reduces how much you can buy with your earnings and savings. Whether inflation gallops or crawls, it steadily cuts your purchasing power. It is the greatest danger an investor faces. Always, you must measure the performance of your investments after subtracting for the impact of inflation.

So, like the multiheaded Hydra monster of Greek mythology, risk poses multiple threats. It menaces your investments in many ways. Any individual investment may be imperiled by one or more *types* of risk, and in varying *degrees* by each.

You'll see it every day in the stock market. No matter how good or bad a day Wall Street may have, some investments move up while others decline, like opposite ends of a seesaw.

MAKE TIME WORK FOR YOU

Often, risk is all a matter of time. If you don't need money you've got tied up in certain stocks or mutual funds right away, you can wait for an investment to recover from a tumble. That cuts your risk. But if you must sell your securities for money to live on right now, you may be forced to sell at a loss. That's risky.

If you can hang tough for, say, 10 or 15 years, you can probably outwait even the most gut-wrenching stock-market setback. And the market recovers from most setbacks much quicker.

Look what happened after the Crash of 1987. The stock market plunged 508 points on October 19, declining 22.6 percent. U.S. stocks lost $500 billion of their value that one day. It was the pathetic low point of a two-month rout in which the Dow Jones Industrial Average (a popular measure of stock-market performance) declined by 36 percent.

But if you had bought stocks then, when prices hit the bargain basement, you would have seen their prices return to their precrash peak in merely 22 months. In another nine months you would have been sitting on top of 5 percent *profit*.

RISK TOLERANCE

As President John F. Kennedy said, "Life is unfair." In the ring, boxers are warned to keep their guard up at all times—even after the bell ends each round. For investors, Wall Street is no less risky.

The question is, How much of that risk are *you* willing to tango with for a chance to win the big dance contest? Exactly how much risk can you stomach before you lose sleep at night? Before you lose your appetite? Before your start biting your fingernails?

Once you determine your level of risk tolerance, you can ask yourself the next question: "What types of investments are right for me? Cautious ones? Moderate-risk ones? Aggressive?"

To help measure your level of risk tolerance, take the multiple-choice quiz in Figure 5.1.

The quiz—like risk tolerance itself—gauges such factors as your income, desire and ability to continue to earn income at a job, job security, marital status, number of children, and spending goals. At the end of the quiz, add up the points for each answer and see your risk-tolerance profile and to which investment style your score corresponds:

1. When it comes to investing in stocks or mutual funds, how would you describe yourself?

(1) Very inexperienced

(2) Somewhat experienced

(3) Experienced

(4) Experienced and sophisticated

Your answer: ________

2. How long before you need any of your investment money to help pay for an expenditure like a new house? (Feel free to refresh your memory by checking Tables 4.1 and 4.2 in Chapter 4.)

(1 point) Less than two years

(2 points) Two to four years

(3 points) Five or more years

(4 points) You don't need any of it because you can afford your expenditures as well as your investments.

Your answer: ________

3. On October 19, 1987, stocks fell more than 22% in value in one day. If you had invested in stocks or mutual funds that fell by so much in a brief period, you would:

(1) Sell what was left right away.

(2) Sell half of it to cut your losses.

(3) Sit tight and sell none of it.

(4) Buy more of the same at the lower price.

Your answer: ________

4. Which answer below best describes how you feel about the following statement: You prefer investments that don't bob up and down much in value, even though investments like that tend to provide lower returns than investments that fluctuate more.

(1) That's me to a "T."

(2) That's more or less me.

FIGURE 5.1 Measure your stomach for risk.

(3) I don't think I feel that way.

(4) Nope, not me at all.

Your answer: __________

5. You want to contribute a specific amount to help your children or grandchildren with some major financial goal, such as paying for education costs. To accomplish that, you have:

(1) Decided to help, but you haven't started saving or investing money for that purpose.

(2) Started saving or investing, and you know exactly how many more years it will take to build the right amount.

(3) Fully funded a trust or some other savings/investment account for that.

Your answer: __________

6. You are planning at least one major expenditure (such as buying a boat) next summer. You'll pay for it:

(1) Somehow. You haven't figured out the details yet.

(2) By cutting back on discretionary expenses like dining out.

(3) By cutting back expenses and by saving and investing.

(4) With money you have already put aside for this.

Your answer: __________

7. If you inherited $40,000 from a long-lost relative, how would you invest it? Only in:

(1) Treasury bills

(2) Certificates of deposit

(3) A mutual fund that invests in Fortune 500 companies

(4) A mutual fund that invests in the hottest segment of the Internet

Your answer: __________

(Continued)

FIGURE 5.1 Continued

8. Which of the following imaginary mutual funds would you be most likely to put money into? Here's what has happened to a $10,000 investment in each. The one whose:

(1) Worst loss in a single year over the past four decades was $150, and whose best single-year gain was $500.

(2) Worst loss in a single year over the past four decades was $1,000, and whose best single-year gain was $3,000.

(3) Worst loss in a single year over the past four decades was $3,500, and whose best single-year gain was $5,000.

Your answer: ________

9. To invest successfully in the Internet, you'll have to do some homework. Which comes closest to describing how much time, interest, and energy you'd have?

(1) You'd be able to devote no more than one hour each weekend to reading a few newspaper or magazine stories. You'd rather leave the heavy lifting when it comes to research to some Wall Street pro who knows what he or she is doing.

(2) You're prepared to put up to three hours a week into learning how some high-tech machines and online business systems operate and how some stocks are doing.

(3) You're eager to put your degree in electrical engineering to good use and you love this stuff. You read, think, and talk about things related to the Internet every day.

Your answer: ________

10. Which statement best describes the savings and checking accounts you have outside your main retirement nest egg, whether it's a 401(k) plan, a traditional pension plan, or one or more IRAs?

(1) "What savings?"

(2) "It pays my monthly bills."

(3) "It not only pays for monthly bills but also for vacations and emergencies."

FIGURE 5.1 Continued

(4) "Same as No. 3 above. Plus, I have separate investment accounts to help pay for things like my children's college educations."

Your answer: ___________

11. Your rich brother-in-law, who is as honest as a saint, offers you several investment deals. Which would you do?

(1) Invest $1,000 so you can get back $1,100 at the end of a year?

(2) Invest $1,000 with a 50-50 chance you'll lose it all or get $1,750 at the end of a year?

(3) Invest $2,000 with a 50-50 chance you'll lose it all or get back $4,500 at the end of a year?

Your answer: ___________

12. Which was the biggest chance you ever took?

(1) Playing the state lottery

(2) Going to a gambling casino

(3) Quitting your job to start your own business

Your answer: ___________

13. This week the stock market went into a nosedive. Your stocks and stock funds lost 15% of their value. What do you do next?

(1) Cut your losses by transferring your money into a money market fund.

(2) Keep your money where it is and wait for the market to turn around.

(3) Invest more money in stock and stock funds, because their prices are such a good deal now.

Your answer: ___________

(Continued)

FIGURE 5.1 Continued

14. Yesterday the stock market went into a tailspin. Your stocks and stock funds lost 15% of their value. What did you do last night?

(1) Didn't sleep well.

(2) Looked in the newspaper for investments that fell only half as much or less.

(3) Recalled the last time the market crashed and thought about how long it took your investments to recover.

Your answer: ___________

15. If you're still working or before you retired: In case you get laid off you keep enough savings available to cover living expenses for how long?

(1) Up to three months

(2) Up to six months

(3) Up to nine months

(4) More than nine months

Your answer: ___________

16. Your favorite major-league baseball team is undefeated during the last month of the regular season. It is about to play a team that has not won a game in three weeks. You've got a chance to bet $500 on your team, with a chance to win $1,000.

(1) Who cares? You don't gamble.

(2) You split the cost of the bet with one of your friends.

(3) You bet with your own money.

Your answer: ___________

17. (Be honest, now.) If you were 35 years old again and had just inherited $1 million, you would:

(1) Retire and buy a new home.

(2) Quit your job and go back to school.

(3) Keep your job *and* go back to school.

Your answer: ___________

Total points:

FIGURE 5.1 Continued

Now, to determine your level of risk-tolerance, add up your points.

✔ **If you scored 17 to 19 points:**

You show minimal interest in planning your finances and you have faith that the future will take care of itself. Also, you prefer to put your money into accounts where your initial investment either is unlikely to lose value or will pay a predictable rate of interest, rather than into investments that might pay more but involve some risk.

Bottom line: You seem to be a conservative investor. Your answers suggest you do not like financial risk. You would be most comfortable with a low-risk strategy. Internet investments may not be right for you.

Your investment motto: **Better safe than sorry.**

✔ **If you scored 20 to 28 points:**

You want investments that will grow, and you are ready to put up with some risk to achieve that. You're willing to make investments that bounce up and down. You're even willing to invest money in a stock or mutual fund that might lose money for the sake of finding others that make a lot of money.

Bottom line: You are probably a moderate-risk investor. Your answers indicate you're willing to suffer the occasional bruise while putting your money to work. But you won't risk stepping on a killer land mine in order to reach a treasure chest that *might* make you fabulously wealthy. It's okay for you to consider investing in the Internet, but you should invest a major chunk of your money outside the Internet as well. As for your Internet investments, consider leaning toward more conservative ones.

Your investment motto: **Don't put all your eggs in one basket.**

✔ **If you scored 29 to 56 points:**

You seem to understand that achieving greater returns requires taking more risk.

Bottom line: Even if you're in this category, it's okay to invest outside the Net as well as in the Net. It's also okay to invest in larger companies whose entire business doesn't depend on the Internet's prosperity. But in general you approach investing the way Bart Simpson approaches skateboarding: aggressively! Where some investors see danger, you see investment opportunities.

Your investment motto: **No pain, no gain.**

WHAT RISK MEANS IN DOLLARS

Now you know what sort of investor you are. What does that tell you about how much of your investment dollars to stake on the Internet?

Cautious investors would say that 5 percent of your investment dollars is a lot to expose to a risky sector of the stock market that jumps up and down. Sure, the volatility is part of the problem. But for most people the possibility that money could be lost altogether is worse.

Ask yourself this: If you *lost* 5 percent of your money, could you handle that? If you're willing to accept that possibility for a shot at multiplying your 5 percent into a lot more, then 5 percent isn't your ceiling. But if your risk-tolerance score shows that you're a conservative investor and your approach to Wall Street is "better safe than sorry," then consider 5 percent the maximum you should expose to the Net.

Moderate-risk investors can flirt with a higher limit. One yardstick to use in setting your own limit is suggested by John Bogle, the highly respected founder of the Vanguard Group family of mutual funds, whose Vanguard 500 Index Fund is now the most popular and largest fund in the world. Bogle points out that it is difficult for investors, professionals included, to achieve better investment results than the overall market's, year after year. One sign of that is how infrequently a simple majority of nonspecialized, actively managed, stock mutual funds succeed in outperforming the Standard & Poor's Composite Index of 500 Stocks. The S&P 500, as it's known, is one of the most widely followed barometers for the health of the overall stock market, although it's actually a cross-section of the market's largest companies.

The 1990s were great years for investors, right? So lots of regular stock mutual funds should have beaten the S&P 500. After all, that index is merely an average for the slice of the overall market that it represents. But in reality the last time during the 1990s that most funds beat the benchmark was way back in 1993. Usually, the index won, hands down. A majority of the supposedly shrewd pros lost, time and again.

The reason is that successful stock picking is harder than it looks. Fees and taxes make it even more difficult. They're an anchor, weighing down performance the way heavy, painful shoes would slow down an athlete. So Bogle urges individual investors not to bother trying. Instead, they should bet on the winner—the overall market—by investing in a cross-section of the market. One way to do that is through index funds.

The idea is to mimic the overall market. You can apply that to Internet investing by limiting the amount you invest in the Net to the Internet's share of the broad market. Since Internet stocks account for about 16 percent of the market's overall value, you would invest no more than 16 percent of your investment cash in Net stocks or funds. You would invest the rest in other segments of the market.

Other investors are comfortable with an aggressive allocation. One approach is suggested by Robert Markman, head of Markman Multi-Funds. He says, "The Internet boils down to electronic technology. Investing in the Internet means investing in electronics, and electronics are involved with moving information in every industry from retailing to biotechnology.

In Markman's view, all high-tech electronics firms are impacted by the same technological advances that drive the Internet. So if you think of all tech companies as beneficiaries of Internet science, then why not invest in tech firms to the same extent that they account for the overall market? And right now about 29 percent of the entire market is made up of tech stocks. That's how much you could devote to Internet stocks.

Markman himself takes an even more aggressive stance. As an investor, he wants to put his money into the fastest growing companies. That's exactly what technology firms have been. So Markman has about 80 percent of the money in the four mutual funds he runs invested in tech stocks.

That approach is not for everyone. It can be volatile in the short run.

"When I talk about investing in technology, I'm not talking about putting all of your money into two or three stocks," he says. "I'm talking about diversifying across a large number. They would be a wide variety of types and sizes. And a large part of any such basket of stocks won't be around 10 years from now. Their companies will make mistakes and wither, and they will go bankrupt. But overall, I expect technology to be the most profitable part of the market."

Whatever level of investment you choose, this is a highly personal, subjective decision. It requires an honest assessment of your resources and tolerance for market ups and downs—especially the downs.

Remember, your risk tolerance may change as your age, circumstances, needs, and experience do. You may switch to a more aggressive investment strategy or a more cautious one.

For now, the next step is to shape an investment strategy that suits you today.

Chapter 6

Choosing Between Stocks and Mutual Funds

Remember when you got your first bicycle, your first car, your first computer? No doubt it was a thrill. You probably got a big kick using it the first time. Besides the sheer fun of it, it expanded your horizons in ways you could not have foreseen. Sure, you had to work at learning how to use it. But that only made it more satisfying once you got the hang of it. Chances are, the more effort it took, the more rewarding it was in the end.

Learning how to invest in the Internet is similar. Learning any new skill requires some effort. But you're already on your way.

In Chapter 4, you learned to figure out how much you can afford to invest. If you don't have spare money for investing, you learned the necessity of hitting up the boss for a raise—or cutting back spending so investing can fit your budget.

In Chapter 5, you learned how to measure your stomach for stock-market gyrations. That helped you decide how much of your investment money to put into the Internet, and how much to put into tamer parts of the market. Likewise, it showed whether you've got the patience, nerves, deep pockets, time frame, and gumption for putting a lot—or only a little—of your investment money into the least predictable parts of the Internet, whose stocks and mutual funds tend to jump up and down the most.

Now you're ready to decide whether you'll invest in stocks, mutual funds, or both.

THE NAME GAME

Let's start by checking our scorecard and making sure we can recognize the players.

Stock. Stock represents *ownership* of a corporation. Shares of stock are individual portions of ownership. Generally, the allotment you own is proportionate to a company's total amount of stock. For example, if you own 100 shares of a company that has issued 100,000 shares, you own one-thousandth of the company. That's one-tenth of one percent. The price of shares may rise or fall.

Bond. When you buy a bond, you are *lending* money to a borrower. That borrower may be a corporation or a government body like a city, state, or school system. Your borrower is promising to pay back the loan itself (the *principal*) as well as interest for use of your money. Unlike stock, a bond does *not* represent ownership of the company. It's simply an IOU from the borrower to you. Its principal may grow or shrink.

Mutual fund. A *bundle* of stocks, bonds, and other securities managed by investment professionals. They *pool* your money with other peoples' and use it to make various investments. You *purchase* shares in the fund. Like an individual company's stock, the price of mutual fund shares is determined basically by dividing the number of shares into the market value of what the fund owns.

Facts of Life

A basic fact of Wall Street life is that stocks and stock mutual funds typically generate much larger investment returns over time than bonds and bond funds. So why doesn't everyone simply invest in stocks and stock funds? Because some investors want what bonds and bond funds do provide: steady income, short-term predictability, and a smooth ride.

Bonds and bond funds pay interest. That's nice for folks whose priority is current income. That explains why bonds and bond funds are so popular among retirees, who commonly don't have a big, steady paycheck any more.

Bonds and bond funds also provide income at regular intervals, typically monthly, typically starting right away. And the prices of bonds and bond funds fluctuate—if at all—much less than the prices of stocks and stock funds.

In exchange for those three much-prized benefits, bonds and bond funds tend not to provide as much overall investment return as stocks and stock funds. In contrast, your compensation for taking a chance on the uncertainty and delayed reward of stocks and stock funds is a shot at a larger overall investment return.

Now, one of our assumptions is that readers of *Getting Started in Internet Investing* are more interested in building wealth for the future than in generating current income. So, most of our discussion will focus on investing in stocks and stock mutual funds.

Besides, many Internet companies are young and raise money for themselves more often by issuing stock than by selling bonds. They can offer investors a shot at shares whose value may rise, without having to deplete their own corporate coffers by paying interest on bonds. Like human youngsters, they need all the energy they can get. They'd rather plow any profits back into growth and expansion.

So, as an investor, you will find it much easier to find Internet stock than bonds.

WHAT'S IN IT FOR YOU

Your goal as an investor is the same, whether you put your bucks into stocks or funds. It is to make money. Basically, you do that in two ways: the price of shares you own rises, or the shares pay you dividends. Many do both.

The changing price of shares and income they pay together are called *rate of return.*

Stocks and mutual funds have other things in common, but there are also differences between them. (And the two of them are quite different in most ways from bonds. More about that later in this chapter.) Because of those differences between stocks and funds, selecting between one or the other involves trade-offs.

Basically, mutual funds are easier to invest in and safer in several

Rate of return Rate of return describes an investment's growth (or loss). It includes how much a stock, bond, or mutual fund's shares rise or fall in price. It also consists of any interest, dividends, or other income paid by the investment. The price change plus income is stated as a percentage of your initial investment or the value of the investment at the start of a specified period, such as the calendar year. The percentage rate change typically tells you how much an investment has grown or lost on an annual basis.

ways. However, their safety features create problems too. It's like trying to hit a long tee shot in golf while wearing football shoulder pads and a helmet. The equipment protects you (well, if you were playing football it would). But it prevents you from swinging your driver as effectively as Tiger Woods.

Take a look at the comparative advantages of owning individual stocks or mutual funds.

Advantages of Mutual Funds

The first advantage you benefit from is the research and stock selection skills of a professional investment manager. This is no penny-ante issue. Having access to an investment manager is the sort of perk once affordable only by Robber Barons. The profits they piled up building railroads, steel mills, and oil empires enabled them to pay for costly professional advice, which they used to earn additional fortunes on Wall Street.

Now mutual funds make that luxury available to you. You get a fund manager's years of experience, his or her insider's access to new stock from hot companies, his or her Big-Money access to valuable intelligence about this or that stock, the expertise of his or her team of analysts, and the number-crunching prowess of their collection of supercomputers. And being able to rely on that frees you to focus on your own rat-race job—unless you happen to be a latter-day Robber Baron.

The second advantage of investing in funds is the built-in diversification. Funds own shares in many stocks—usually at least 20 to 25, and most hold 50 or more—which spreads your risk. Your eggs aren't in a single basket. If one or more stocks' shares crash and burn, other stocks in the fund's portfolio (its collection of stocks) are likely to remain stable. That protects the value of your shares in the fund itself even when one or a few of its stocks get into trouble.

Third, it takes less work to own mutual fund shares. Internet investing calls for an aggressive approach. Individual stocks that you've bought should be sold and replaced by faster-growing stocks. If you invest directly in stocks, you've got to pay attention to how they're doing and watch for attractive replacements. That takes time and effort. But mutual fund shares don't have to be bought and sold nearly as frequently. The fund itself buys and sells stocks as their prospects ebb and flow. The fund does much of the work that otherwise would fall on your shoulders.

Conservative investors will tell you that investment strategies for individual stocks and for mutual funds should be the same. This is one of those areas where investing resembles hot-stove league discussions about baseball. In those mid-winter bull sessions, everyone has a different opinion about what it takes to produce a winner. Our bottom line: any sort of Internet investing is risky. But investing in Internet stocks requires an even more aggressive approach than investing in Internet mutual funds. We'll elaborate in Chapters 12, 13, and 14.

Fourth, buying funds is convenient. In most cases, all you have to do is call a fund or fund family's 800 number. You can find those toll-free numbers in the mutual fund tables in many newspapers and magazines. They're also posted at fund web sites. You can also arrange to buy shares at the web sites themselves. And you can buy shares through mutual-fund supermarkets, like those run by Charles Schwab & Co. and Fidelity Investments.

It's not difficult to buy shares of stock either. But the wider variety of ways to buy fund shares makes them a tad handier.

Fifth, in many ways it's easier to select a fund than to choose individual stocks. Funds have public track records. They tell you in advance what their investment targets are—whether it is the Internet overall, a specific segment of it, or something else altogether. And it's often easier to gauge the prospects for a broad swath of the market than for an individual company.

It's certainly easier to misjudge a single company, or for a single company to deviate from what's expected of it. In a fund portfolio, unexpected results from one stock won't throw off the group's overall performance as much. Further, a fund manager's record, preferences, and strategies are as well known as the history and tendencies of individual large-company executives.

Finally, mutual funds can be less expensive to own than stocks bought through a broker. Sales commissions and annual fees on funds can cost you less than commissions on stock purchases at full-service and some discount brokerages.

Fees and Expenses

Mutual fund commissions are known as *loads*, and they're commonly charged when you buy or sell shares. If you invest $1,000 in a fund that charges a 5 percent load, for instance, $50 of your money is sidetracked to a salesperson. Only $950 goes to work for you in your account.

Some funds are known as *no-loads* because they don't charge any commission. You can typically buy their shares directly from the fund family, using a toll-free 800 phone number.

Despite their name, some no-load funds charge a commission of as much as 3 percent or 4 percent. These are called *low-load funds*. Be sure you understand whether a fund truly is no-load.

Loads can range up to 8.5 percent. In addition, funds can levy a management fee and other operating charges. These costs are reflected in a fund's *expense ratio*. Even a true no-load fund may charge shareholders such costs. The average expense ratio for stock funds is about 1.4 percent. If you invest $1,000 in a fund with an expense ratio of 1.4 percent, you'll pay that fund $14 per year to manage your money.

Some funds impose much lower expense ratios. The Vanguard 500 Trust Fund (which is not an Internet fund; it invests in the Standard & Poor's 500 index, a cross-section of the stockmarket's largest and steadiest companies) is famous for its penny-pinching 0.18 percent expense ratio. Because it simply mimics the investments in the S&P 500, which doesn't require a lot of expensive analytical brainpower, its costs can be low.

Most Internet specialty mutual funds charge more. Unlike Vanguard 500 Trust, they don't have a play book handed to them. They've got to explore for winners. And most aren't part of large fund groups, so they can't share research expenses with other funds. Right now Munder NetNet, Firsthand e-Commerce, Goldman Sachs Internet Tollkeeper, and Enterprise Internet have expense ratios ranging from 1.5 percent to 1.95 percent, says Lipper, Inc. Another, Monument Digital Technology, has an expense ratio of 2.763 percent. Unified Select Internet's expense ratio is a penny-pinching 0.35 percent.

But costs by themselves should never be your focus. Your primary goal should be to find an investment whose returns are superlative. High returns more than pay for high fees. It's how much you put into your own pocket at the end of the day that matters.

Whatever size an expense ratio is, you'll never get a bill for it. Instead, the fund deducts the fee automatically from the value of your shares every day. An annual fee that size, plus a low or zero load, will cost you less than most brokerage commissions on individual stock. Only a few of the deepest discount online brokerages, whose sales commissions are in the single digits (or which offer free trades to eligible investors), charge less to buy stocks on a per-transaction basis.

Pluses of Stocks

Now look at the advantages of investing in individual stocks.

First, you can get a more dramatic investment return investing in stocks. That's because you're *not* spreading your risk. Your return from one fast-growing stock won't be diluted by the lower returns of other stocks, which is what happens with a mutual fund. Of course, this assumes you've bought shares in an especially fast-growing stock. Buy shares in a company that takes a nosedive, and just the opposite happens: You get walloped by a declining stock.

Second, you get greater control over your investments. You can invest in the specific stocks and segments of the Internet that you prefer. If you happen to be a telecommunications engineer with a feel for your industry, you can target companies you know best. A fund might spread your investment dollars over other industries or even telecom companies you don't want. No such problem with individual stocks.

Third, if you enjoy researching stocks and get your jollies buying and selling, individual stocks give you opportunities to do just that.

Fourth, there are fewer stocks than funds to choose from. With about 8,100 mutual funds available (excluding various share classes of the same fund), funds outnumber stocks on the New York Stock Exchange by almost two-to-one. That staggering number of fund choices stymies most people. Bedazzled, investors become like deer frozen by the headlights of an onrushing car. And doing nothing is the worst choice an investor can make.

Fifth, you avoid built-in tax booby traps. When you buy shares in a mutual fund, you join other shareholders in being responsible for the tax burden on shares owned by the fund itself. Here's how that tax liability builds up: As each stock the fund owns increases in value from its original purchase price, there's a tax on that appreciation once the fund sells the shares. Its profit on those shares is called its *capital gain*. If the fund owns the shares for a year or less, you are taxed on the capital gain at your ordinary income-tax rate. For example, if you're in the 28 percent tax bracket, that's the rate you pay on your portion of the fund's profit on the sale of these stock shares. That's known as the *short-term capital-gains rate*.

If the fund owns the shares for more than 12 months, the rate is usually only 20 percent. This *long-term capital-gains rate* gives you a built-in tax break. It's always less than your ordinary income-tax rate. If you're in the 15 percent tax bracket, long-term capital gains are taxed at only 10 percent. This is Uncle Sam's way of encouraging people to invest for the long haul.

In either case, guess who actually pays that tax. You and other shareholders pay almost all of it. And it doesn't matter how long you owned your shares in the fund. Even if you bought your fund shares only one day before the fund sold its shares, you're responsible for a portion of the tax burden in proportion to the number of fund shares you own. If you own, say, 1 percent of the fund's shares, you're credited with 1 percent of the capital gain at whichever tax rate applies.

So, you could get stuck for your portion of the tax burden whether or not the fund shares themselves go up in value. Worst of all, you get a cap-gains tax bill even if the fund shares go *down* in value while you own them.

Taxes: A Burden They Have in Common

Like the capital-gains tax liability that's built into ownership of mutual fund shares, you're also responsible for cap-gains taxes on shares in the fund itself. But since the same rule applies to stock shares, it doesn't tip the scale in either direction in terms of the debate on the merits of mutual funds versus stocks.

Still, learning about this will help you better understand investing in funds and stocks overall. If you buy shares in a fund or individual stock for a low price and sell them for a higher price, the difference is your capital gain. You pay taxes on it the same way you do on cap gains distributed by a fund. In other words, if you held shares a year or less before selling, your gain would be taxed at the ordinary income rates. But if you held them more than 12 months, your gain would be taxed only at the favorable long-term rate. This rule applies in the same way to shares of mutual funds and stocks.

In addition, there's another type of potentially taxable income you can receive from a mutual fund or from individual stocks. Some stocks and bonds pay dividends. Likewise, a fund will distribute to you dividends paid by stocks and bonds it owns. Whether you are paid directly as an investor in the stocks and bonds themselves or indirectly as a

Tax relief You get a free pass, exempting you from yearly taxes on capital gains or dividends, if you own a fund or stock shares inside a tax shelter like a 401(k) plan or an Individual Retirement Plan (IRA). You don't have to pay taxes on dividends and capital gains paid to your account as they occur year by year. You only pay taxes at your ordinary income-tax rate when you *take money out of a tax-qualified plan.*

fund shareholder, you are responsible for taxes on this at your ordinary income-tax rate.

By the way, all of those types of income—increases or decreases in share prices, capital gains, and dividends—contribute to the total return from a fund.

Taxes are bad news. But investors got one good piece of news on New Year's Day. As of January 1, 2001, some capital-gains rates began to go down. For investors in the 15 percent federal tax bracket, the new long-term rate is 8 percent, replacing the old 10 percent rate. But to get the lower rate, you must hold the investments for more than five years.

If you own an investment less than five years but at least 12 months, your sale profits will still be taxed at the old 20 percent capital-gains rate. If you're in the 15 percent bracket, your profits will be taxed at the 10 percent rate.

If you are in a higher income-tax bracket, your cap-gains tax rate drops to 18 percent from the old 20 percent—but only on investments you obtain after December 31, 2000, and hold more than five years.

The new rules apply to capital gains on shares in the fund sold by you or on shares in securities sold by the fund. But they don't apply to interest or dividends paid by the fund.

MAKING YOUR CHOICE

You can invest in individual Internet stocks if:

- ✔ You're a control freak.
- ✔ You prefer to focus only on a few investments or only on individual companies.
- ✔ You enjoy working without a net.
- ✔ You're prepared to invest the extra hours required to research and track individual stocks.

Making your own investment decisions can be fun and satisfying, especially if you simply don't enjoy relying on someone else's investment moves.

Moveover, investing in individual companies gives you a shot at dramatic returns from stocks that skyrocket, without having your returns diluted by less-spectacular stocks that you would also own as an investor in a mutual fund.

But the flip side is true too. If you rely on only a few individual stocks and they tank, you don't have the protection that a fund's diversification provides—no safety net. And if you invest in individual stocks, you'll have to do the research that a professional manager and his platoon of analysts would do for a mutual fund.

We're not trying to persuade you *not* to invest in individual stocks. We simply want you to understand the risks and rewards.

You should probably stick to mutual funds if:

- ✔ You're a newcomer to investing.
- ✔ You place a priority on ease, saving time, simplifying your choices, and cutting your risks.
- ✔ You'd rather restrict your research and decisions to seeking funds that are best for you, while leaving the stock-picking to an investment pro.

If you have any doubts about which type of investing would suit you best, err on the side of caution and start out with funds. Get your feet wet, see how much appetite for research you truly have, and gauge your stomach for risk-taking. You can always shift into individual stocks as time passes.

In fact, this does not need to be an either/or choice. You can invest in both. Consider that as we discuss investment strategy first for funds, then for individual stocks, in the following chapters.

Chapter 7

Basics of Internet Investing Through Mutual Funds

Sure, Internet investing through mutual funds is easier and less risky than investing directly in individual stocks. But that doesn't mean Net investing through funds is a no-brainer. Just the opposite. There's a rapidly growing number of Net funds, and you can bet the ranch that at any given moment their investment performances are wildly divergent.

Through the first eight-months-plus of 2000, for example, Strong Internet Fund was the front-runner. Bringing up the rear was Jacob Internet Fund. In this trying period for Internet funds, Strong was the leader by virtue of having lost the least amount of ground: 2.9 percent, according to Lipper, Inc., a fund-tracking firm. Meanwhile, Jacob Internet lost more than 53 percent in that time. The average return for all Internet funds tracked by Lipper was a loss of nearly 20 percent.

Why such a wide range of investment performances? The explanation is that Net funds aren't all alike. They don't invest in the same things. Some aim to reflect the overall industry sector, and their holdings cover a broad spectrum of companies. Newer funds tend to focus on one or more segments of the Net. And there are not only many segments, but a variety of opinions among investment pros about the best bets in each.

We'll look at those various approaches, starting in the next chapter. Meanwhile, let's take a look at the basics of selecting a mutual fund in general. The same rules apply to choosing one or more funds in a sector like the Net.

HANDICAPPING YOUR TEAM

When you think about it, selecting a fund for Internet investing isn't all that different from figuring out your favorite pro football team's chances of winning the Super Bowl this year. Mutual funds and football teams are organized in similar fashion. And placing a bet on either one can be costly, while both can tease you with the tantalizing prospect of a big payback.

It's also very easy to get emotionally caught up with either type of choice. But that's also the surest way to loose your shirt. When it comes to risking your money, the smartest approach is to do what the smart-money crowd does, whether it's on football or a mutual fund. Leave emotion out of it. Bet with your head, not with your heart.

That's the biggest difference between folks who place bets with their neighborhood bookie and guys who move to Vegas so they can wager on sports legally for a living. The guys who pack up and move to Nevada aren't betting on a ball club because it's their old home-town team or because that's where a guy they played high school ball with went to college. They only put their money to work on teams whose prospects they like—based on cold-blooded analysis. Even if it means betting on a club to *beat* their own old college team.

And forget that image implanted in your brain by Hollywood

movies—you know, the one of the dapper guy who spends a leisurely day sitting in a darkened, air-conditioned bar, served drinks by scantily clad waitresses or studly bartenders, until it's time to stroll into the casino so he can place a bet or two. It's hogwash; pure Hollywood fiction.

Professional bettors work hard, poring over details. They do the same thing you must do. Check out the facts. In fact, you're better off than they are. Bettors have got to do it every day, over and over. You've only got to do it periodically with funds. Still, the examination process has remarkable similarities.

ROSTER AND STRATEGY

Funds are as different as football teams. They have different investment strategies, different strengths and weaknesses. Just as some football teams are stronger offensively than defensively, or play better late in the season when the weather turns cold and wet, so too some funds succeed better than others in particular economic environments or market conditions.

The stocks, bonds, and assorted goodies they invest in are their players. And, like team lineups, player personnel can be more talented in some areas than others.

With the potential for so many differences from one fund to another, it's likely that some may suit your needs and interests much more than others. Choose the ones that are right for you. Start by taking the time to understand what a fund's orientation is. The four best sources for information are the fund's name, its prospectus, its web site, and news articles about it.

All in a Name

A fund's name can tell you whether the fund specializes in some segment of the Internet. For example, Internet Infrastructure Fund's specialty isn't hard to figure out. Not every fund's forte is as obvious from its name alone, though. Usually, it takes a little more digging to determine that.

Prospectus and Reports

Your go-to source of information is a fund's *prospectus*. That document tells you everything from a fund's investment strategy to its goals, sales commissions, performance history, and manager.

At first, a prospectus can be hard to read. That's because technically they are legal documents, written by committees of lawyers. (Don't you wish you could join those fun-filled sessions?) But once you thumb through the pamphlet for a while, you'll find sections devoted to each of those topics as well as others. Better yet, government regulators are encouraging funds to simplify their prospectuses. In any case, it's worth the effort because so much information is packed into a prospectus.

Funds typically disclose their lineups in their *annual* and *semiannual reports*. These pamphlets list a fund's portfolio of stocks, bonds, and other investments. The fund shows how much of each security it owns. Also, it lists its 10 largest holdings and often shows how much of each it owned at the time of the previous report, probably six months earlier. (Some funds voluntarily file reports more often.) Further, the fund provides a breakdown of its investments by industry categories, and many compare that to the breakdown as of its previous report. These reports also include the fund manager's diagnosis of what happened to his or her investments since the previous report was issued: why some succeeded while others failed.

All in all, these are key documents. They explain what a fund's game plan is, how well it has executed that plan, and they reveal the fund's roster. These documents are a sort of cross between scouting reports and game-day scorecards. They may not be fun to read, but they are the single most important thing for you to read.

Web Site

You can get a prospectus from the fund itself or, usually, its web site. You can also find fund prospectuses at web sites that specialize in investment documents.

If you want to read a prospectus online or print a copy, you'll have to download it. (For those of you new to the Internet, *download* means retrieving a copy from a storage computer out there in cyberspace. Once you download it, you can read it and, in most cases, print it.)

> **Acrobatic** To be able to download and read or print out a document online, you'll need a program called Adobe Acrobat Reader. You can download a freebie copy of *that* from www.adobe.com/products/acrobat/readermain.html.

Internet New Paradigm is a sibling of Internet Infrastructure Fund. They are specialized Net funds that were opened on the last day of 1999 by Kinetics Asset Management. Kinetics, by the way, is the corporate parent of Internet Fund, one of the oldest Internet funds. It and two competitors opened in 1996.

Unlike Internet Infrastructure, New Paradigm's area of interest is not obvious from its name. If you read its prospectus, you quickly discover that it invests mostly in well-established companies whose basic businesses are not rooted in the cyberspace. But what does this have to do with the Internet?

The answer is right there on the fund's web site. Among the fund's largest holdings in the first half of 2000 were businesses like the Washington Post and Chris-Craft Industries. Washington Post owns not only a newspaper and *Newsweek* magazine, but also TV stations and a cable system among other things. Chris-Craft Industries—the former boatbuilder—has left the water world and taken to the airwaves with its majority ownership in a string of TV stations. One subsidiary also makes plastic

Edgar

Mutual funds (as well as individual companies that are traded on stock exchanges) must file regular reports with the Securities and Exchange Commission (SEC), which is Uncle Sam's primary regulator of the investment world. That paperwork is stored in a database with the unwieldy, bureaucratic name Electronic Data Gathering, Analysis and Retrieval. Its nickname is Edgar.

If you're a glutton for punishment, you can look up documents on the SEC's web site. Navigating the site can be difficult, and filings are in rough-to-read raw form.

Far better are sites run by Edgar Online (www.edgar-online.com) and by FreeEdgar.com (www.freeedgar.com). One company owns both services. Edgar Online charges a fee for access, but offers advanced research tools. You can read prospectuses and annual and semiannual reports for free on the FreeEdgar.com location.

film products, such as water-soluble laundry bags, primarily for the chemical and health care industries.

As the fund manager explains on the web site, New Paradigm is betting that those and other companies in which it is investing are using the Net to significantly expand the sales of their products, services, and ideas.

Flipping through pages on Kinetics's web site, you can learn more about New Paradigm's other two Net-specialty siblings, also founded at the end of 1999: Internet Global Growth Fund, which invests in foreign and domestic Internet companies, and Internet Emerging Growth, which invests in the venture capital and incubator firms that finance Internet startups. You'll also see additional vital data about each of the funds. For instance, you can get periodically updated lists of companies in which the funds invest. You can check each fund's asset size, which gives you some idea about how popular a fund is with other investors—in other words, how good other people think the fund is. You'll find basic information like its daily price, whether it charges a sales commission, and how you can buy shares in it.

News Publications

Your next step should be to check out news articles. They are like reports prepared by an independent football scouting combine, not your team's own scouting staff. As outsiders, they give you a fresh perspective. Theirs is a neutral viewpoint. That freedom to tell the truth as they see it is their key benefit.

It's essential to learn what you can from official information on web sites and in prospectuses and other valuable documents. In the *annual* and *semiannual reports*, for example, the fund manager identifies which of his or her investments worked and which flopped recently and why they turned out that way.

But nothing beats the unvarnished analysis of what a fund is doing right and wrong that you can get from outside sources such as newspapers and magazines. A fund's own look back at recent winners and losers is usually annoyingly brief. That's natural. No one likes to dwell on shortcomings. And many funds don't want to elaborate on triumphs, either, for fear of building shareholders' expectations so high that they can't be satisfied again.

In contrast, press accounts can be longer and more detailed, and can point out more connections between causes and effects. In short, press accounts can paint a clearer picture of what—if anything—a fund's past says about its future prospects.

It's increasingly easy to find your favorite news publications online. But watch where you step in cyberspace. Always ask yourself whether you are doing homework at a web site produced by a news or financial-services organization with a tradition of reliability. Or are you reading material posted by an organization with a vested interest in selling you something?

Likewise, when you are reading material called *news* in an Internet discussion room, ask yourself what you know about the people who posted or provided that information. Some web *chat rooms* or sites devoted to financial topics feature honest opinions by honest people. There's nothing wrong with an opinion. But opinion doesn't equal fact. There's nothing wrong with a web site or its participants having points of view. Just be sure you understand what they are. (More dangerous: Some articles may be posted by people with a financial interest in encouraging you and others to invest in particular companies.)

Take everything with a grain or two of salt. Always ask yourself why you should trust anything you're reading.

HEAD COACH

The portfolio manager is head coach of a fund. He or she sets the overall tone for the fund. It's the manager who oversees how the fund tries to achieve its strategy. The buck also stops with the manager in terms of deciding which investments to make.

A fund may have scouts and specialty coaches. Those are its own or its parent company's researchers. But what if one or more make conflicting recommendations? What if their recommendations are wishy-washy? What if they're young and the manager isn't sure how much to trust their judgment? What if they make more shrewd and persuasive purchase recommendations than the fund can afford?

It's the manager who must decide whether to pull the trigger and spend the fund's cash on a particular stock. It's also up to him or her to decide which holdings to trim or eliminate to make room in a fund's portfolio for stocks with better prospects.

So how do you judge a manager? First, you want a winner. Look up the fund's annual performance. How has it done in the years the current manager has had the helm? If he's managed another fund, look up his track record there too.

You can find that information in newspapers and magazines, in a fund prospectus, on a fund web site, or from services like Value Line or Morningstar, via their printed and online reports.

In a relatively new realm such as Internet investing, most managers won't have long track records within this industry sector. But many have been at it long enough to show what subsectors of the Net they know best and how well they can do. And if a manager has consistently posted losses or lagged his competitors, that's a red flag.

Just remember not to mistake a manager's lackluster performance during one of the market's periodic downcycles for an outright lack of stock-picking skill. For example, Jacob Internet Fund lost 79.1 percent during all of year 2000. The S&P 500 lost "only" 10.1 percent. Should you avoid any fund run by the manager of Jacob Internet?

Not unless you're willing to do without the stock-picking services of Ryan Jacob. Before starting his own mutual fund, Jacob ran the Internet Fund. In the 18 months during 1998 and 1999 he was at its helm, the fund racked up a scorching cumulative return of about 517 percent. That was nearly double his closest rival, according to fund-tracker Morningstar Inc., making him the Mark McGwire of the fund world. And that may well be part of the reason you want to learn how to invest in the Internet yourself.

His aggressive tactics can produce breathtaking results over the long haul. But in the short run, you must be willing to put up with a nerve-wracking rollercoaster ride.

TEAM PERSONALITY

Some football teams are known for their passing game, others for their running game. Some teams are built around defense, others depend on offense to win.

Funds are similar. It's impossible for a fund to be excellent at all things. The market is too big and too diverse. Not all stocks go up at once. Not all sectors of the market thrive at the same time. Market conditions evolve. The economy keeps shifting.

So the sort of fund you invest in has a lot to do with your chances for success. If, for instance, telephone manufacturers offer better wireless phones than ever before, and consumers start to buy them in unprecedented numbers, then telecommunications companies sign up record numbers of wireless-phone subscribers. Funds with lots of wireless stock will do well. A year or two or three later some other niche may be hot.

Some investors believe it is simply too hard to figure out which individual stocks will benefit the most from constantly changing market and economic conditions. They prefer to bet on the prospects for industry sectors or groups of stocks instead. They invest in funds designed to do that by focusing on a particular segment of the Internet industry. They're called *index funds*.

An index is a set group of Internet stocks, chosen to illustrate the performance of a selected cross-section of the Internet. The index may be broad, cutting across the entire Internet. Or it may be narrow, focusing on just one or more subsectors such as infrastructure.

Index funds are known as *passive* funds because they do not rely on active choices of stocks. The portfolio is preset by the index the fund tracks. The manager is not making independent stock choices, and his or her role is relatively unimportant.

In contrast, the manager of an *actively managed* fund is making decisions about buying and selling stocks all the time. The manager is not relying on a preset group of stocks. Instead, the manager is free to choose from all Internet stocks.

An active manager can do that by trying to figure out which sectors of the Internet are hot, then choosing stocks he or she thinks are most likely to capitalize on that trend. (This is known as *bottom-up analysis*.) Or an active manager can ignore or downplay broad trends and instead look for individual stocks, regardless of what industry sector they're in, whose earnings are growing dramatically and whose stock price should follow suit. (This is called *top-down analysis*.)

It's helpful to understand the different approaches taken by funds. But you're not restricted to one or the other. You can invest in either, or you can invest in some from each category.

THE REST OF THE LEAGUE

Football teams don't stay the same. Players, whether they are superstars or benchwarmers, age or fall victim to injury. Other teams find better players. Strategies grow stale. Competitors figure out better ways to win.

So it is with mutual funds. Longtime all-star stocks stop producing stellar returns. Obscure startup companies become the new heroes. Fund managers must adjust by changing their portfolio lineups, or the fund's performance will lag and fall behind in Wall Street's never-ending competition.

Like all industry sectors, the Internet will evolve. Its subsectors will go through cycles of prosperity, growth, overcrowding, and consolidation. Companies engaged in electronic retailing earned colossal returns in 1999, so much so that they attracted more and more competition. That proved the undoing of all of them. There weren't enough retail customers to go around. Companies were forced to battle each other by slashing prices. And, finally, e-tailers began to go broke.

In contrast, during 2000 companies helping to build the Internet have remained relatively healthy. Companies helping to build the infrastructure of wireless telecommunications, which has applications outside the Net as well, have remained especially attractive to investors.

Nothing stays the same. Once-great stocks fade. Newcomers start to shine. New technologies emerge, making new sectors hot. Once-promising technologies are made irrelevant by something better.

Sometimes a natural aging process takes place. Formerly hot industry sectors cool off as they mature. That happens as a few companies emerge as leaders in their respective business niches. Their small competitors from previous years fade or die. The surviving leaders enter a sort of corporate middle age. They produce steady profits, but less than when they were young. The spectacular growth of their early years disappears. If you want rapid, dramatic growth—and you should—you must look elsewhere.

FIELD CONDITIONS

Over time, the market rises and falls. Sometimes the overall economy is strong. Sometimes the stock market is in retreat.

As you consider what funds specialize in and how they've performed, look at how they've performed in various market conditions. Like football teams that play well only during warm, sunny weather, some funds only gain ground when the Fed is lowering rates or when certain industries are prospering.

Ask yourself not only whether a fund has been hot, but in what conditions it has been hot. And are those conditions likely to repeat themselves?

A WINNING TRADITION

Some pro football franchises rarely make it to the big dance. Others form dynasties, repeating year after year or at least advancing far enough to challenge for a shot. When injuries or retirement of key players take their inevitable toll and the team finally sags, the entire organization seems to buzz with eagerness to return to greatness. What follows are calculated steps: new players, new coaches, whatever it takes to make it back to the top.

It's not all that different with a fund. Stick with winners that know how to win over the long haul. Even if they suffer periodic setbacks, they know how to bounce back. Don't bet on funds that don't know how to win. Betting on a fund that gets lucky and wins once is like betting on a broken clock. Even if its arms don't move, it shows the correct time twice a day. But that doesn't make it any good.

Likewise, never, ever choose a fund or manager solely on the basis of recent, short-term performance. A one-year performance record is not long enough to provide a persuasive indication of how a fund is likely to do in the future.

In any case, past performance is no guarantee of future results by any sort of mutual fund, let alone one specializing in this volatile industry sector. A brief period of performance is even more unreliable as a barometer of the future.

A three-year track record is more useful. Unfortunately, few funds in this sector have existed that long. In this volatile section of the stock market, it is at least equally useful to bet on the tendencies of subsectors rather than expect an individual fund or manager's past to point reliably to future performance.

TICKET PRICES AND SIX-BUCK BEER

Most football fans have a love-hate relationship with their favorite team. They love the team itself, but they hate the business of sports. They hate star players holding out for zillion-dollar pay raises. They hate benchwarmers earning multimillion-dollar contracts. And, to pay for those abominations, they *really* hate escalating ticket prices, $30 parking-lot fees, $5 hot dogs, and $6 watered-down beers.

Nevertheless, most of them keep attending games or watching on TV. Until, that is, their team tanks. Then attendance or TV audience share slips because fans decide the end result is no longer worth the costs.

Mutual-fund shareholders face a similar trade-off. The want a winning fund with high returns. But they don't want to pay high sales commissions, management fees, expenses, and taxes.

Yet Internet funds have costs that are higher than the typical stock fund's. As we saw in Chapter 6, several Internet funds impose higher-than-average sales commissions. The aggressive nature of Internet investing means funds buy and sell their stocks frequently, generating hefty taxes on the profits from those sales. And because many Internet funds are not part of large fund families, they must absorb higher administrative overhead costs with less help from corporate siblings. That boosts their expense ratios.

But should you care? Well, it's like those six-buck beers at the football stadium. If your team is going to Super Bowl, coughing up the cash hurts less. Likewise, so long as Internet funds can produce superior returns, their higher costs hurt less. In fact, a lot less. The only thing that matters is how much you take home at the end of the day (or, more likely, the end of the year or two or three or five).

Suppose an Internet fund is charging you, say, $19 a year in operating costs for every $1,000 you've invested, while the typical general stock fund would charge you only $14. It's well worth the cost if the Net fund is doubling your $1,000 that year, while the general stock fund is only earning you an extra $250.

Do you really want to trade in your $750 advantage for the sake of saving $5? Of course not: For every dollar you earn from the fund, your cost is actually much less than it is in the average stock fund.

In a way, that makes you more like one of your football team's overpaid, pampered players than an exploited fan!

EXPERIENCE COUNTS

Past performance is not a guarantee of future success by a fund. It's notoriously futile to put money into a fund that was hot last year, expecting it to repeat automatically.

But one thing that does help a fund is managerial experience. It's not that a veteran can simply retrace his steps to end up with the same success he's reached before. It's more that experience teaches a manager how to navigate treacherous shoals.

Sure, experience helps make a manager a better stock-picker. But experience really shows its value when trouble strikes the market. An experienced manager can minimize losses during a market downturn.

An experienced manager knows where hazardous eddies swirl, where dangerous reefs lurk, and where the safest harbors are.

Experience also confers an edge among Net investors because most Internet funds are so young. Most of their managers don't have extensive experience managing Net funds or even technology-focused funds of any sort.

Here's a look at some funds blessed by exceptional manager experience—and one that illustrates the Net sector's lack of experience:

- ✔ RS Internet Age Fund is comanaged by Jim Callinan and Cathy Baker. Callinan was honored as Domestic-Stock Fund Manager of the Year in 1999 by Morningstar, Inc., the fund-tracking service. He won that honor not for overseeing an Internet fund, but for his stewardship of RS Emerging Growth Fund, which gained nearly 183 percent in 1999. In comparison, the S&P 500 (which is a barometer for the market's large, strong stocks) advanced a relatively puny 21 percent that year. In its own right, a 21 percent return is good—in fact, it's very good. But RS Emerging Growth far outdistanced that index.

  Callinan has managed Emerging Growth since July 1996. He has shared the helm of RS Internet Age since the end of 1999. He also gained experience picking smaller stocks, which many Internet stocks are, when he ran Putnam OTC Emerging Growth Fund from mid-1994 to mid-1996.

  Meanwhile, his Internet Age copilot Baker has been the Internet analyst for RS Emerging Growth since early 1997.
- ✔ Enterprise Internet Fund is managed by David Alger. With a staff of about 20 analysts, eight of whom specialize in technology stocks, Alger successfully runs a flock of stock funds. He's been at the helm of some more than a decade.
- ✔ Firsthand e-Commerce Fund is part of a fund group based in Silicon Valley, specializing in technology. Kevin Landis is man-

ager. He runs four other tech-oriented funds. He's overseen Firsthand Technology Value, one of the most successful funds focusing on technology stocks, since May 1994.

- ✔ Goldman Sachs Internet Tollkeeper is led by Herbert Ehlers and teammates. Ehlers is a member of teams running nearly a dozen other funds, some with hefty stakes in tech stocks. His tenure at Heritage Capital Appreciation Fund, which did better than the market overall 1997 through 1999, dates back to 1985.
- ✔ Amerindo Technology technically isn't an Internet fund. In its prospectus, it does not declare that its strategy is to target the Net. But in fact most of its money is invested in the Internet, and it is widely perceived as a Net fund. The two versions of this fund (one is for regular retail investors; one is available only for institutional investors, like members of certain retirement plans) gained an astounding 250 percent in 1999. Manager Alberto Vilar heads a team that has been investing in technology for about 20 years.

  The Vilar group has introduced a fund named Amerindo Internet B2B, which targets stocks using the Internet in their dealings with other businesses.
- ✔ Monument Digital Technology Fund racked up a 273 percent return in 1999, while Alexander Cheung was at the helm. The fund's parent company reportedly had only one analyst, though, and Cheung left in late March 2000. The fund's lack of managerial depth doesn't mean it will perform badly. In fact, it is no worse off than most Internet funds. As with those other Net funds, if you put money into this fund you can't do it on the strength of longtime experience.

WELCOME TO THE GAME, ROOKIE!

In football, winning and losing start with mastery of the fundamentals. Players start over in training camp each year to learn their team's plays and refresh their athletic skills. Heck, rookies must learn where the practice field itself is.

So, too, newcomers to investing must learn the basics of buying fund shares:

- ✔ You can buy shares either from the fund or through a fund supermarket. To buy directly from the fund, call its (usually) toll-free number or visit its web site (see Table 7.1). Ask the sales representative for an application, or fill out a request for one. You may be able to fill in an application right at the web site.

  Also, the fund is required to send you a prospectus. At the web site, you may be able to start checking the fund's investment goals, sales charges, annual expenses, performance record, and manager history.

  We've listed some vital stats in Table 7.1. Bear in mind that funds may impose other charges, such as a fee if you sell your shares within a certain period of time like 12 months.

- ✔ If you need to wait for an application and prospectus to arrive by mail, fill it out when it arrives and return the application with your check. Minimum initial investments in nonretirement accounts generally range from $250 to $10,000. Subsequent investments usually may be in smaller amounts.

  A high initial minimum investment is often a sign that a fund wants to cut its own expenses by discouraging a lot of smaller accounts. It may also signal that a fund wants to discourage casual investors who may not be prepared for the wild market gyrations of the Internet sector.

  If the fund charges a commission on the purchase of shares (called a *front-end load*), it will subtract that fee from the amount credited to your account. Check Table 7.1 to see how large each fund's front-end load is.

  Funds set the price of their shares at the end of each business day. That's the price, called *net asset value* (NAV), you see listed in mutual fund tables in newspapers and magazines.

Table 7.1 Buying Shares in Internet Funds

Fund	Ticker Symbol	Front Load	Expense Ratio	Minimum Initial Purchase	Phone	Web Site	Manager
Amerindo Internet B2B	BTBAX	5.75%	2.09%	$2,500	888-832-4386	www.amerindo.com	Alberto Vilar, Gary Tanaka
Enterprise Internet	EIFAX	4.75%	1.83%	$1,000	800-368-3527	www.enterprisefunds.com	David Alger
E*Trade E-Commerce Index	ETECX	0%	0.95%	$1,000	800-786-2575	www.etrade.com	Team
Firsthand e-Commerce	TEFQX	0%	1.95%	$10,000	888-884-2675	www.firsthandfunds.com	Team
Goldman Sachs Internet Tollkeeper	GITAX	5.5%	1.5%	$1,000	800-526-7384	www.goldmansachs.com	Team
Investec internet.com Index	IINTX	0%	1.98%	$2,500	800-915-6565	www.investecfunds.com	Doug Blatch, Domenico Ferrini
ING Internet	INGAX	5.75%	2.24%	$2,000	877-463-6464	www.ingpilgrim.com	Guy Uding
Internet	WWWFX	0%	2.00%	$1,000	888-386-3999	www.kineticsfunds.com	Peter Doyle, Steven Tuen
Internet Index	N.A.	3.0%	1.4%	$2,500	800-234-0849	www.igam.com	Eugene Lee

Investors Capital Internet and Technology	N.A.	5.75%	3.0%	$250	877-423-8637	www.investorscapital.com	Thomas Fitzgerald Jr.
Jacob Internet	JAMFX	0%	2.00%	$2,500	888-522-6239	www.JacobInternet.com	Ryan Jacob
Monument Digital Technology	MFITX	5.75%	1.9%	$1,000	301-215-7550	www.monumentfunds.com	Bob Grandhi
Munder NetNet	MNNAX	5.5%	1.66%	Closed to new investors	800-438-5789	www.munder.com	Team
Potomac Internet Plus	PNETX	0%	1.5%	$10,000	800-851-0511	www.potomacfunds.com	Team
Potomac Internet/Short	PDISX	0%	1.65%	$10,000	800-851-0511	www.potomacfunds.com	Team
RS Internet Age	RIAFX	0%	1.83%	$5,000	800-766-3863	www.rsim.com	Jim Callinan, Cathy Baker
WWW Internet	WWIFX	0%	2.5%	$2,000	888-263-2204	www.internetfund.com	Lawrence York, James Greene

This table data shows you the basics of what you need to know for investing in these Internet funds. Included are phone numbers and web sites for reaching the funds and obtaining applications and prospectuses. The table also shows the minimum size your initial investment must be. Each fund's manager is listed, and so is the sales commission and yearly expense ratio.

Note: Information applies to A-class shares.

Data Source: Fund companies.

✔ If you're going to invest in more than one fund, you may find it more convenient to buy shares in them through an account at a fund supermarket. Charles Schwab, Fidelity, and others run supermarkets where you can buy shares in funds run by them as well as their competitors. (Schwab and Fidelity don't happen to operate any Internet funds of their own.)

The steps you'll need to take are similar to those required if you buy directly from a fund. Get an application, fill it in, send a check. Once the supermarket receives your money, you can buy and sell shares.

Chapter 8

Internet Funds Aren't All Alike

Not long ago, it was far easier to tell Internet funds apart. First of all, when the sector sprang into existence, there weren't that many funds. The first was born in 1996. The first two were born within weeks of each other that August. The next two were born within seven days of each other in October. By the dawn of 1998 they were still the only Internet-fund game in town, and they outperformed the rest of the market dramatically.

In 1999 they did even better. The Internet funds turned in mind-blowing triple-digit returns. But that triggered a stampede of investors, rushing in with fresh cash. As a result, by late 2000 there were 64 versions of 25 Net funds, including a number of very new and small funds, according to Lipper, Inc. Even more are on the drawing boards.

That makes it much harder to tell one fund from another.

It's not just the number of choices you face. It's difficult to choose because the funds perform very differently. The key to choosing an Internet fund is understanding what those differences are and why they can be so large. Once you understand those differences, you can select one or more funds based on how you want to invest.

You can choose funds that invest the way you want to. You can avoid the rest.

HOW MUCH DO THEY DIFFER?

Internet funds have differed from each other all along. Compared with the rest of the stock market, they move in a pack. But like lions on the hunt, they sometimes spread out. Still, there's no problem telling them apart from the animals in the herd.

In 1997, as a group the young funds badly lagged behind the rest of the stock market, as Table 8.1 shows. After all, they were investing in a lot of young companies with scant or zero profits. Individually, the funds' dissimilar records illustrated differences in their respective investment approaches.

In 1998 they turned the tables on the rest of the market, sensationally outperforming other stock funds and most other investors. But, still, there were big gaps among the Internet funds themselves. One Internet fund did better than twice as well as the rest of the stock market. The best of the four Net funds that year did six-and-a-half times better than the rest of the market! Likewise, there were jumbo differences among the Internet funds themselves again in 1999, when they smoked the rest of the market.

While the overall market gained more than 21 percent for investors—about double the historic yearly rate of return—two Internet funds advanced 167 percent and 176 percent respectively. That means, of course, that every dollar you put in earned an additional $1.67 and $1.76. Plus, you still owned your original dollar. In a bank account, you would have been lucky to earn 2 or 3 cents on your dollar. Better yet, that same year the Internet Fund, run by Kinetics Asset Management, scored a staggering 216.44 percent gain. Amerindo Technology Fund grew an astonishing 248.86 percent.

Table 8.1 Internet Funds' Performance

Fund Name (earliest share class)	*Date Fund Began*	*Performance* 1997	1998	1999	2000 (through Aug. 10)
Amerindo Technology (D)	10/28/96	–18.11	84.67	248.86	–28.85
Kinetics Internet	10/21/96	12.74	196.14	216.44	–30.21
Munder NetNet (A)	8/19/96	30.43	97.96	175.65	–13.54
WWW Internet	8/1/96	0.43	70.47	167.03	–22.47
Internet-fund category average[1]		6.37	112.31	206.19	–19.7
S&P 500 Index		33.4	28.6	21.1	–1.8

The S&P 500 Index is a barometer for a big part of the overall stock market. Internet funds have moved in a loosely packed group, performing very differently from the rest of the stock market, represented by the S&P 500. But no two Net funds perform identically because each follows its own strategy.

[1]Category average based on nine funds in 1999. In 2000, category average calculation based on 33 funds.

Source: Lipper.

Obviously, the Internet was a realm where a lot of investors wanted to put their money to work. It could grow as rapidly as mold on week-old biscuits. Equally obvious is that some stocks in the Internet were growing faster than others.

The question asked by many investors is: How do you spot one or more funds that are betting on the fastest-growing stocks?

Sibling funds

In Table 8.2 and elsewhere in *Getting Started in Internet Investing*, several funds have the same name, followed by different letters. Those letters—commonly A, B, C, and so on—represent different versions (called *share classes*) of the fund.

One (often the A share class) in each such name group is the oldest. You can tell which that is by the starting dates in the third column. Often, the oldest is the largest in the group. The others are basically clones of the original.

Various versions or share classes typically impose different fees on investors. The A class of a fund, for example, commonly charges a sales commission at the time you buy shares. The B class generally levies a commission at the time you sell them instead.

Commissions are reflected in a fund's performance. But because commissions vary in size and timing, various share classes of the same fund can have slightly different returns.

Sometimes, one version is open only to specific investors, such as members of 401(k) plans. Other share classes are available to other investors.

TIME IS MONEY—THEN AND NOW

The question as to which funds have the fastest-growing stocks is crucial, no matter when you ask it.

In 1999, when the market was user-friendly, the gap between the best and the worst funds was an eye-popping 81 percentage points. Just that difference alone would double your investment in little more than one year!

Even in 2000, when the technology companies were in a severe

Table 8.2 Internet Funds' Performance Comparisons

Fund Family and Fund Name	*Fund Size (in $ millions)*	*Date Fund Began*	*Return %*		
			Jan. 1–Aug. 10, 2000	*3 Years Ending Aug. 10, 2000 (annualized percentage rate)*	*From Fund Inception Through Aug. 10, 2000 (annualized percentage rate)*
Amerindo Technology (A)	23.0	8/7/98	–28.85	N/A	94.98
Amerindo Technology (D)	442.0	10/28/96	–28.85	62.51	37.94
Analysts Internet	2.1	5/4/99	–8.47	N/A	23.45
Enterprise Internet (A)	167.5	7/1/99	–12.88	N/A	152.92
Enterprise Internet (B)	172.7	7/1/99	–13.07	N/A	151.94
Enterprise Internet (C)	58.2	7/1/99	–13.17	N/A	151.69
Enterprise Internet (Y)	1.0	7/1/99	–12.62	N/A	154.32
Firsthand e-commerce	501.6	9/30/99	–17.09	N/A	23.2
Goldman Sachs Internet Tollkeeper (A)	1050.0	10/1/99	–6.44	N/A	98.59
Goldman Sachs Internet Tollkeeper (B)	960.0	10/1/99	–6.82	N/A	97.05
Goldman Sachs Internet Tollkeeper (C)	551.0	10/1/99	–6.83	N/A	96.92
Goldman Sachs Internet Tollkeeper (I)	158.0	10/1/99	–6.08	N/A	99.49
Goldman Sachs Internet Tollkeeper (Svc)	N/A	10/1/99	–6.45	N/A	98.34
Investec internet.com Index	38.5	7/30/99	–16.08	N/A	50.95

(Continued)

Table 8.2 Continued

Fund Family and Fund Name	Fund Size (in $ millions)	Date Fund Began	Return %: Jan. 1– Aug. 10, 2000	Return %: 3 Years Aug. 10, 2000 (annualized percentage rate)	Return %: From Fund Inception Through Aug. 10, 2000 (annualized percentage rate)
ING Internet (A)	83.0	7/1/99	–32.6	N/A	51.02
ING Internet (B)	50.0	7/1/99	–32.8	N/A	49.98
ING Internet (C)	25.0	7/1/99	–32.84	N/A	50.06
ING Internet (X)	5.0	7/1/99	NA	N/A	56.86
Jacob Internet	116.2	12/13/99	–53.07	N/A	–67.81
Kinetics Internet	819.3	10/21/96	–30.21	91.1	66.45
Kinetics Internet Emerging Growth	9.4	12/31/99	–35	N/A	–50.64
Kinetics Internet Global Growth	19.6	12/31/99	–14.2	N/A	–22.2
Kinetics Internet Infrastructure	17.8	12/31/99	–20.1	N/A	–30.77
Kinetics Internet New Paradigm	3.1	12/31/99	–10.1	N/A	–16.01
Mercury Internet Strategies (A)	0.1	3/22/00	N/A	N/A	–59.57
Mercury Internet Strategies (B)	0.1	3/22/00	N/A	N/A	–59.87
Mercury Internet Strategies (C)	0.1	3/22/00	N/A	N/A	–59.87
Mercury Internet Strategies (I)	0.1	3/22/00	N/A	N/A	59.57
Merrill Lynch Internet Strategies (A)	141.6	3/20/00	N/A	N/A	–58.01

Merrill Lynch Internet Strategies (B)	383.7	3/20/00	N/A	N/A	–58.32
Merrill Lynch Internet Strategies (C)	225.0	3/20/00	N/A	N/A	–58.32
Merrill Lynch Internet Strategies (D)	94.1	3/20/00	N/A	N/A	–58.01
Monument Digital Technology (A)	113.4	11/3/98	–25.23	68.17	109.54
Monument Digital Technology (B)	23.9	10/4/99	–25.44	N/A	43.97
Munder NetNet (A)	2911.4	8/19/96	–13.54	72.76	68.58
Munder NetNet (B)	3323.8	6/1/98	–13.96	N/A	85.37
Munder NetNet (C)	1661.2	6/1/98	–13.93	N/A	102.06
Munder NetNet (Y)	27.3	6/1/98	–13.44	N/A	87.38
RS Internet Age	211.8	12/1/99	–12.15	N/A	10.29
Rydex Internet (Adv)	65.6	4/3/00	N/A	N/A	–54.16
Rydex Internet (Inv)	7.0	4/3/00	N/A	N/A	–54.67
StockJungle Pure Play	0.7	11/17/99	NA	N/A	–13.6
Strong Internet Fund	89.4	12/31/99	–2.9	N/A	–4.71
Unified Select Internet	2.4	4/7/99	–19.47	N/A	19.29
WWW Internet Fund	N/A	8/1/96	–22.47	44.94	41.17

This list shows performance by selected funds over various periods of time. The fifth column shows how these funds fared in 2000 through the first 10 days of August. The sixth column shows how they did in the 12 months that ended August 10, 2000. The next column shows each fund's average annual gain in the three years ending August 10.
The size of each fund as of July 31, 2000 is shown in column two. The third column lists the starting date for each fund. "N/A" means not available, typically because the fund did not exist for the entire time period.
Source: Lipper.

slump, there was still a gap of 50 percentage points between the best- and worst-performing Net funds through the first eight months of the year.

Table 8.2 shows the incredibly wide variety of results produced by some Internet funds that have been around long enough for Lipper, Inc., a fund-tracking service, to post them. No matter which time period you look at, the funds overall performed differently from one another. Obviously, some did a much better job than others at finding the few Net stocks doing well at that time.

Aren't those the ones you'd want to put your money into?

Chapter 9

How to Tell One Internet Fund from Another

Okay. Some Internet funds do better than others. So how do you spot the winners?

It boils down to this: Differences in performance aren't random. Those differences stem from how funds are run and what they invest in.

Go back to some things you learned in Chapter 7, when we discussed how to spot differences among funds. We compared funds to football teams. We explained that funds can have different personalities. One team may have slow running backs but a quarterback who's a whiz at passing the ball long. Not surprisingly, that team builds its offense around passing. Another team may be blessed with ferocious linebackers, who crush an opponent's running game. The team focuses on stifling the opposing teams and on getting good field position for scoring points.

It's the same with mutual funds. Strategies are built around a fund's strengths and weaknesses. A fund is likely to excel at picking stocks in an industry or industry sector that the fund manager and the fund's analysts know best. Maybe they once worked in that sector. Maybe that was the first sector they researched when they got a job as an investment analyst. Perhaps it's a sector they find personally fascinating. Whatever the reason, that's where their analytical skills are strongest. They can spot stocks to buy before anyone else, and they're the first to know when to sell.

Repeatedly, they do a better job than others at buying low and selling high.

MORE BRANCHES ON THE FAMILY TREE

Unfortunately, it's not always easy to tell one fund's strategy from another. And it's getting harder. Differences among funds are growing.

The original four funds all lagged behind the overall market in 1997. While the S&P 500 index, a widely used barometer for the market, advanced more than 33 percent that year, the Net quartet gained an average of only 6.37 percent. After all, they were investing in stocks of many young companies that were struggling to get off the ground. And few other investors cared about these stocks, so there were few other buyers to buoy their share prices.

In 1998, while the rest of the market gained nearly 29 percent for investors, three of the four original Net funds gained between about 70 percent and 98 percent. Compared to the typical slowpoke fund investing in the rest of the market, the three were in the same general high-octane neighborhood. (The fourth, the Internet Fund, was in a league of its own. Its 196 percent return was a hair better than double its closest rival's.)

The same thing happened in 1999. By year's end, the nine funds in the sector (the original four plus their own new *share classes*—basically, clones of the first four) enjoyed returns ranging from about 167 percent to a stratospheric 273 percent. Their average was a shade better than 206 percent. The overall market, meanwhile, gained a little more than 21 percent—decent, but Little League compared to the Internet funds' major-league effort.

Those comparable performances by Net funds were evidence of a generally similar approach to investing. Although the funds don't perform identically because they are not copy cats when it comes to choosing their investments, their investment strategies share certain key features.

They approached the Net as if it were an investment buffet. They sampled a wide variety of its goodies, plucking some here, tasting some there. Most of all, they shared an appetite for young, fast-growing companies.

In contrast, new Net funds are increasingly specialized. More focus on just a single aspect of the Internet. Some concentrate on infrastructure companies. Others aim for electronic retailers. Whatever one or more categories such funds hunt, their strategies depend on buying stocks in those categories. In the end, the fund manager must make a choice to buy some stocks and not others. Likewise, periodically the manager must decide which stocks to sell and which to hold.

As we explained in Chapter 7, that's called an *active* stock-picking strategy. But not all funds use an active strategy. Some use a *passive* stock-picking strategy. That's how index funds typically work.

Several new Internet funds are index funds. Like active Internet funds, they may stalk only one slice of the Net pie. Some target a cross-section of the entire Internet industry. But these broad index funds are still a far cry from the original four Internet funds.

Unlike those first four, the holdings of index Net funds commonly don't change often if at all. They invest in a fixed list (or index) of Internet stocks. The index fund invests in those stocks in the same proportions as their weightings in the index. In other words, if one stock accounts for one-quarter of the value of the whole index group, funds that mimic that index will put one-fourth of their money into that one stock.

An index is usually created to serve some purpose. It may be to help investors or analysts keep track of the overall health of the Internet. That's the goal of the ISDEX, an index featuring 50 leading Internet companies, such as Amazon, Yahoo!, and Cisco Systems. They reflect almost 80 percent of the Internet's entire value, says Investec Asset Management, which runs the index.

Other indices monitor the ups and downs of a specific segment of the Internet. The most popular segment currently is wireless communications. A year from now it could be something else.

In any case, an index fund generally depends much less on shrewd stock-picking. All it has to do is hold onto the stocks that its index carries.

PLANTING THE FLAG

Why have funds bothered to specialize? The trend stems from three things, Internet-fund expert Jason Burr says:

1. Economic ability.
2. Marketing motivation to distinguish themselves from each other.
3. The reward for a fund being among the first to plant its flag in a new territory.

Burr explains them this way. A fund needs to manage about $10 million to $25 million before it can hope to break even. It needs that much money to pay for its own startup costs and ongoing overhead. Funds in large mutual-fund groups need less money to reach break-even because they can share their costs with their siblings.

As each Internet fund got off the ground in 1996, it needed to attract enough money to survive. That required appealing to the widest possible audience. And until it pulled in enough investor money, it couldn't afford to deviate from that approach.

Now a few Net funds have grown so much they individually hold roughly 100 to 200 times more money than that $10 million minimum. Many others are well beyond that basic threshold as well. The problem is no longer lack of investor familiarity. In fact, investor interest has triggered a proliferation of Internet funds. Now the challenge is how to stand out from the crowd. The best way to catch shareholder dollars isn't by casting a wide net. Just the opposite. It is by specializing. That lets each fund build a unique identity.

And with so many Internet funds rushing into the marketplace, managers need to establish their identity and lure a following of investors as soon as possible. It's simply easier to hold onto new territory if you're among the very first to colonize it. After you plant your fund's flag, your marketing team can beat their drums and draw investors' attention, and there's little or nothing to distract them from you and your flag.

"It's simply a matter of building brand recognition," says Burr. "Being first at something can be rewarded significantly."

FIVE PIGEONHOLES

You can pigeonhole Net funds many ways. But many experts agree that Net funds fit into half a dozen or fewer categories.

Jason Burr, a specialist in Internet investments and a founder of MAXfunds.com, a web site that analyzes Internet funds and small funds in general, says Net funds fit into five groups: wireless communications, business-to-business (B2B) and enabling technologies (often called *infrastructure*), New Economy, index, and general.

The number of categories may grow slightly with time. Eventually, enough funds may focus on, say, security software for that group to deserve its own category. Or the categories may stay the same but more Net funds may specialize, shifting from the general category into one of the niche categories. In any case, this trend marks a departure from the relatively homogenous approach in 1997 taken by all four of the first Net funds.

On the other hand, the number of fund categories is much smaller than the dozen or more categories that investment analysts use to describe individual Internet stocks. That's because funds still can't afford to pigeonhole themselves too narrowly.

"If a fund did that, it would risk restricting itself to investments in a small number of stocks," says Burr. "That's fine if those stocks are hot. But it can be a problem if those stocks go cold. Diversification gives funds a wider margin of safety." Basically, it lets them avoid putting all of their eggs into one small basket.

Why have the four niche categories (plus the general category) that Burr sees emerged, rather than others? Those are where funds think they stand the best chances of finding winning stocks.

YOU CAN'T RECOGNIZE THE PLAYERS WITHOUT A PROGRAM

The five categories of Internet funds are fairly broad, and each includes stock from a wide range of companies. Take a look at each group.

Wireless

Wireless focuses on the part of the telecommunications industry that uses radio signals rather than ground wires to send voice and data transmissions. Basically, it is the industry catering to cell phones. But wireless communications also involves pagers. Some simply tell you you've got a phone call with a friendly wiggle in your pocket. Others display brief messages.

Wireless telecom also includes personal digital assistants. PDAs display information, but they are much more powerful than pagers, have bigger screens, and can show more information. They resemble pocketsize minicomputers much more than pagers do. You can choose among various channels, as if you were surfing the Web on your desktop computer.

Even now, while PDA technology is relatively crude, you can use one to do everything from catch up on network news to consult a map, fish through your Rolodex for names and numbers, and check your calendar.

No wonder wireless is popular. And it's growing. The number of wireless communications subscribers worldwide leaped to 478 million in 1999 from 309 million the year before, says the investment firm Credit Suisse First Boston. It was projected to balloon to 680 million in 2000 and then to nearly double to 1.16 billion by 2002.

That's a lot of people signing up for cell phones, PDAs, and pagers of all shapes, sizes, functions, and formats. Telephone companies are drooling at the prospect of selling them voice service. And companies that sell data are champing at the bit too.

Consider just one, brokerages. They are spending big bucks so customers can conduct investment transactions, peek at stock prices, or merely check the status of their accounts no matter where they are—on the beach, in a car driving to work, stuck in some distant airport.

The effort appears to be paying off. Fidelity Investments, the Boston-based financial giant, for example, began simply. It offered customers stock quotes via wireless devices in October 1998. Actual trading via wireless started three months later.

By April 1999, Fidelity had a modest 2,100 wireless customers. But within two months the number of wireless subscribers nearly doubled to 4,046. It more than doubled again by September of that year to 9,618. By the end of that year, 27,566 customers were trading online and managing their accounts with their wireless devices, according to Fidelity's figures. The ranks of wireless subscribers doubled again, reaching 56,227 by the end of March 2000. Two months later Fidelity's wireless rolls had climbed to 63,150.

Fidelity happens to be privately owned. But its size makes its wireless numbers highly visible and easy to understand. And competitors like Charles Schwab and E*Trade with publicly traded stock are scrambling to capitalize on the same trend.

There's certainly plenty of room for growth. Dramatic as the growth of wireless activity is, it's still a mere penny in the coin jar compared with overall investment volume. Fidelity alone had 11.4 million retail accounts as of the end of July 2000. Its wireless customers make up barely one-half of one percent of that total.

So who else are all of those new wireless customers? They include soccer moms, who want to be able to reach the babysitter on a moment's notice. They include delivery-truck drivers, who want to reach customers whose address they can't find. They include junior executives, who want the boss to be able to bug them any time of day or night. They include Hollywood moguls, who want to be able to reach other moguls sitting three tables over at trendy restaurants.

That's why, while financial services firms can only day dream about the *potential* of wireless, other types of companies already are seeing a real return on their investment dollars. And if the wireless industry is a modern gold rush for investors, then companies scoring profits today are those that make the picks and shovels used by the gold miners.

Those include companies like Nokia, which makes cell phones. Another wireless company is Qualcomm. The San Diego-based company used to make cell phones, but it has sold that business to Japan's Kyocera. The company remains a leader in the manufacture of computer chips used in cell phones.

In fact, in Chapter 10 we'll look at the actual holdings of several Internet funds. You'll learn more about how one fund differs from another. And you'll see how professional investors build portfolios of individual Net stocks.

B2B and Infrastructure

Let's play some more with our gold-rush metaphor. Question: If cell phones and the chips inside them are the picks and shovels of the Internet, what sort of companies make the steel tracks and iron carts that ferry ore in and out of mines, then away to distant factories?

Answer: infrastructure companies.

Burr puts infrastructure and business-to-business companies into a single category: "Enabling-technologies companies all do business with other businesses. They are business-to-business companies," says

Burr. "It doesn't matter to me whether they do some of their business *on* the Internet. Their goal as a business is to build the Internet. That gives them a financial stake in the Internet."

So mutual funds in this category invest in everything from regular B2B companies to infrastructure companies.

In turn, B2B firms span a wide range. Some harvest only a fraction of their revenues from the Internet. The rest reap all or at least the bulk of their revenues from the Net.

Ditto for infrastructure companies: Some gain a lot of their business by selling picks and shovels to corporations mining the Net. Other companies sell most of their picks and shovels to companies digging for gold elsewhere.

In both groups, companies that do only a small part of their business online are more likely to be known to the general public. That's because they were born well before the Net, and they've become familiar fixtures of the corporate landscape because of their traditional, offline activities.

Take the Big Three auto makers, Ford Motor, General Motors, and DaimlerChrysler. They joined the ranks of B2B companies when they announced in February 2000 their formation of an online exchange for car parts.

The same month United Technologies and Honeywell International said they would launch MyAircraft.com, a web site for aerospace parts and services. Airlines and manufacturers of aircraft equipment would be partners.

Likewise, steel makers Bethlehem Steel, LTV, Weirton Steel, and Steel Dynamics forged an electronic exchange for supplies in 1999. USX's U.S. Steel Group became a 5 percent owner of e-Steel, a rival exchange, in 2000.

Compare that roster of household names to companies that are pure B2Bs. That is, they only do business on the Net with other companies. For instance, do you know about Noosh, which is a matchmaker between businesses that need something printed and printing companies? Or BBQ.com, which said it wants to run an exchange for makers of grills, smokers, sauces, and meats? It is hardly a lock that any of these will grow into household names.

Then there are infrastructure companies. Again, some of the players are familiar. Those companies include the likes of Lucent Technologies (which once upon a time was Ma Bell's Bell Labs unit) and Nortel Networks (the former Northern Telecom). Those two are the Bobbsey Twins of telecom-equipment making, the biggest and second-largest in their manufacturing field. High-tech devices they make are used in everything from phone-center switches to wireless equipment, broadband network systems, fiber-optic systems, and e-business software and services. About the only pieces of the global telecom skeleton they don't have a big hand in are telephone poles.

Cisco Systems is another key player in the world of backroom gizmos that keep the Internet humming. This San José, California-based company's jaws are locked on more than three-quarters of the global market for products that link networks and power the Internet, including routers and switches. You'll recall from Chapter 3 that this is the equipment that shuttles data around the Internet and corporate networks. No routers and switches, no Internet.

And not content to rest on its laurels, the company has taken aim on the market for telecommunications equipment and optical-based systems that have long been big breadwinners for competitors Lucent Technologies and Nortel Networks. With such bright success and future ambitions, small wonder that this company's stock was, as mentioned in Chapter 3, the best-performing of any on Wall Street during the decade of the 1990s.

Infrastructure, though, is not limited to big, heavy things made of steel, silicon, and miles of fiber-optic cable. Products that enable other companies to do business online include computer programs. And right now the leading provider of software that automates the sales and customer-service operations of big businesses is Siebel Systems.

Its software is the brainpower behind online operations for companies whose customers reach them through lines laid on the ground or via wireless transmissions. And its own customer roster includes heavyweights like Lucent Technologies, Prudential Insurance, and Glaxo Wellcome, the giant drug-maker.

New Economy

The Old Economy includes traditional companies that are taking advantage of the Internet to expand their business and revenues. Their names definitely do not end in dot-com. You may not even know that they have begun to stick their toes into the Net pool. But they are busy finding ways to grow by doing business online.

Generally, they are not infrastructure companies. They have not been lured by the prospects of helping to build the Net. Rather, they are using the Net to do more business. In that sense, they are B2B or business-to-consumer (B2C) companies, but not the variety created expressly for the Internet. And, unlike many B2B companies, they do not simply operate online exchanges for buying and selling components of one or more end products. Those B2B companies keep right on doing what they've always done. They merely use the Net to cut costs and speed up various procedures.

Likewise, New Economy companies have their roots in the Old Economy. What distinguishes them is that they are using the Net to transform and enhance themselves. As an example, Burr cites W. W. Grainger, a leading distributor of maintenance and repair supplies to businesses and institutions. What could be more Old Economy than bolts and buckets, lightbulbs and mops, wax and washing fluids?

But Chicago-based Grainger is using New Economy technology to protect its market dominance, expand revenues, and help customers improve their own businesses. It is doing that by investing in several web sites, which help companies do business with each other as well as with Grainger.

At TotalMRO.com, for example, customers not only can identify, select, and purchase MRO products and services, but they also can get industry news provided by leading trade journals. That helps customers stay on top of the latest trends and techniques in MRO. Naturally, that alerts them to new products and services, which they can obtain from Grainger.

"This is a company using the Internet to become more than they were in the past," says Burr. "They build from an existing business platform, and explore new business worlds."

Grainger's strategy may prove successful. But in the meantime it entails risk. The firm's online sales grew 400 percent in the first half of 2000, according to *Investor's Business Daily*. But it seemed as if professional Wall Street investors could only worry about the cost of those added sales. The company's stock price fell 50 percent from March through mid-October. Toward year's end, though, the stock had regained about half its loss.

Lesson: Using the Internet to expand sales is nice. But the cost of that campaign must pay off in higher profits. That's the challenge taken up by Grainger, and by every company that attempts this expansive—and expensive—strategy.

Index

The easiest way to discuss this category is in terms of the funds that fit in rather than the stocks they invest in. That's because there's no single type of index. An investment firm can create an Internet index to serve as a barometer for the overall health of the Net or of any segment of it.

As we discussed earlier, the two most common forms of index funds are those that track the Internet overall and those that track its wireless sector. Of course, funds that have the same goal may go about doing it differently. If they choose different sets of stocks to serve as proxies for the entire Internet, there's a good chance their performances will vary from each other.

That's exactly what happens. The investment results for several such Internet index funds vary. We'll take a look at these later in this chapter and discuss why.

General

This is simply a catchall category for any funds that don't fit neatly into one of the four niche categories above. Funds whose investments range widely around the Internet fit this grouping.

FUNDS BY CATEGORIES

Now that you've got a handle on how to tell one fund category from another, let's take a look at which funds fit into which categories.

Just don't expect all funds to fit conveniently into one and only one category. That's because the world has been irritatingly imperfect since Adam and Eve were booted out of the Garden of Eden. As a result, not all of the questions you ask have black-and-white answers. In the case of Internet funds, it means some funds are hard to categorize. Others may fit into more than one category. Still more may switch from one category today to another tomorrow, like some sort of investment-world chameleon. A fund may be hard to pigeonhole because its investments span a variety of Net categories. Generally, such a fund fits the general category.

Figure 9.1 shows funds that most clearly fit one of the five Net-fund categories, according to Jason Burr. The listing includes some brief thumbnail commentary about the category by Burr.

Some funds make it easy for investors to understand their focus. The segment of the Internet that they invest in exclusively or heavily is part of the fund's name. In Figure 9.1, it's obvious from their names which funds focus on the wireless sector of the Net, which specialize in business-to-business companies, and which target infrastructure companies.

Kinetics Asset Management started no less than four specialty funds on the last day of 1999. The fund family's Internet Infrastructure Fund's name is self-explanatory. Its New Paradigm Fund goes after companies that are part of the New Economy.

Wireless

This category is like an intersection of telecommunications and Internet funds. The category includes:

- Investec Wireless World Fund (IWWDX)
- Profunds Wireless Communications UltraSector Fund (N/A)
- Turner Wireless and Communications Fund (TIWCX)
- Value Trend Wireless Fund (WIREX)

B2B and Enabling Technologies

Some of these funds call themselves B2B, which makes them easy to identify. Others reflect this in their holdings. The category includes:

- Amerindo Internet B2B Fund (BTBDX)
- Firsthand e-Commerce Fund (TEFQX)
- Kinetics Internet Infrastructure Fund (WWWIX)
- Turner B2B E-Commerce Fund (TBTBX)

New Economy

These funds invest largely in offline companies that are taking advantage of the Internet and its impact on our society. The category includes:

- Investec Wired Index Fund (IWTRX)
- Kinetics Internet New Paradigm Fund (WWNPX)

Index

These funds attempt to create an index, which reflects the health of the overall Internet economy or a segment of it. The category includes:

- E*Trade E-Commerce Index Fund (ETECX)
- IGAM Internet Index Fund (N/A)

General

This category includes most of the large Internet funds that charge a sales commission or load. "That's because load funds have a large sales force behind them, so they don't need to differentiate themselves by specializing in one segment of the Internet," Burr says.

- Goldman Sachs Internet Tollkeeper Fund (GITAX)
- Kinetics Internet Fund (WWWFX)
- Monument Digital Technology Fund (MFITX)

FIGURE 9.1 Internet Funds by Category.

This listing shows which categories many Internet funds fit into. Each fund's ticker symbol is in parentheses, to make it easier for you to look it up. N/A means the fund has not been given a ticker symbol yet. Nasdaq symbols are typically assigned when a fund reaches $10 million in assets.

Source: Jason Burr, MAXfunds.com.

The group's Internet Global Growth Fund invests in companies around the world that are seeking to capitalize on the Internet. In some ways the most daring of Kinetics's new funds is its Emerging Growth Fund. What makes this fund adventuresome is that its objective is to invest in companies that are mere startups. The growth potential of such corporate pups is enormous. But the risk is that young companies are vulnerable to lots of dangers, such as ruthless competition and the modest resources typical of small businesses.

Other funds' names give no hint of whether they specialize and, if so, where. What in the world, for example, is the Goldman Sachs Internet Tollkeeper Fund (and its various share classes) about? Its name sounds lyrical. But what does *Tollkeeper* refer to, anyway?

As it turns out, the prominent money-management firm Goldman Sachs has something specific in mind. The name is not poetic whimsy. It is, in fact, meant to alert investors to the fund's mission. In Wall Street parlance, *tollkeepers* are formidable companies whose very size and might serve as roadblocks to potential competitors.

Here's how Goldman Sachs describes it: "[Our] approach to Internet investing is to buy Internet Tollkeepers—established growth businesses that are strategically positioned to benefit from the expansion of the Internet. What is an Internet Tollkeeper? Internet Tollkeepers are companies with recurring revenue streams that often dominate markets with high barriers to entry. Like a toll collector for a highway or bridge, tollkeeper companies may grow revenue by increasing 'traffic,' or customers and sales, and raising 'tolls,' or prices."

In other words, Goldman Sachs doesn't care what part of the Internet a company exploits. The decisive factor to this fund is that the company is an established market leader, which can't be pushed around by competitors. Newborn dot-coms need not apply.

A footnote: You don't need to be a personal acquaintance of the Goldman Sachs corporate historian or even one of the firm's brokers to find out about the fund's investment likes and dislikes. As *Getting Started in Internet Investing* has been emphasizing, the key to making investment decisions is knowing how to gather information and understand it. All of these explanations about funds' names and strategies are posted on their web sites or are printed in prospectuses or periodic reports.

The key to making investment decisions is time: taking the time to gather information, then taking the time to digest it.

And don't worry about the Wall Street jargon. We'll translate. In fact, this book is even better than your old high school French-to-English dictionary. It's like a sharp-edged knife. It's great for cutting through the gobbledygook.

Chapter 10

Which Internet Fund Should You Buy?

As we've discussed in preceding chapters, Internet funds don't all perform alike for the simple reason that they don't invest exactly like each other. *Getting Started in Internet Investing* has described how the funds *do* invest. In fact, many funds' investment tendencies fit into categories. Now that we've defined, described, and delineated them, you can tell one category from another.

But that's just the appetizer. It's time for the main course, so let's carve up the turkey. What are each sector's prospects for making you rich?

MAKING MONEY OFF THE BUILDOUT

In large part, it depends on what your time frame is.

In the near future, professional investors like infrastructure companies. Their logic: The Internet is still being built, so there's still lots of demand for picks and shovels.

"If I had to say which Internet sector held up better in the market downturn during the year 2000, I'd say it's the infrastructure sector," says Peter Doyle, chief investment strategist for Kinetics Asset Management, which runs Kinetics Internet Fund and its four younger sibling funds. "And since the Internet, as a business tool, is not going away, companies providing the picks and shovels for construction of the Internet will continue to have more stable revenues, higher revenue bases, and more earnings than many dot-com companies."

The question investors, whether they are part-time investors like readers of this book or full-time professionals like Doyle, must ask is how long that buildout will continue: "It's kind of like the coming of the railroads or telephone systems or electricity," Jeff Provence, manager of Value Trend Wireless Fund, said in an interview with the MAXfunds.com web site. "For the first 20 or 30 years, they were the place to make money." After that, those industries entered corporate middle age. Their businesses grew at much slower rates. Revenues and earnings flattened.

Things move faster, though, at the start of the twenty-first century than they did at the end of the nineteenth century and early years of the twentieth century. Few experts expect the buildout of the Internet to continue at breakneck speed for two or three decades. Prime time may lose its spark in only a year or two.

On the other hand, major but unforeseeable technological innovations could force businesses to keep upgrading. Corporations could be forced to replace one generation after another of Net infrastructure. The penalty for failing to keep pace would be obsolescence and defeat. Like it or not, companies would have to keep spending on infrastructure. The buildout would go on for many years, like a perfect surfers' wave crossing a vast ocean.

In either case, you'll know when the buildout is petering out. Watch for share prices in infrastructure funds to slow their growth. Ditto for individual stock prices. (More about individual stocks, starting in Chapter 11.) Make a list of two infrastructure funds and six of the leading stocks they invest in or others you select. Use those as *your* barometer for the infrastructure sector. If they all start to lose steam—especially if the rest of the stock market and the technology sector in general are doing okay—you'll know the party is over.

How much steam? If that sector loses 30 percent or more, the jig may be up.

WIRELESS: ANOTHER NEAR-TERM FAVORITE

Wireless is a category by itself, although very broadly speaking it is part of the infrastructure buildout. As we've discussed, wireless rates its own category because it is where so much of the buildout action is.

Investors, though, simply aren't sure how long the wireless craze will keep growing as fast as a teenage brontosaurus. The key reason for those cautious doubts: Are there enough people clamoring for wireless phones and devices? Are there, in fact, enough additional people who absolutely, positively *can't* resist trading securities while they're waiting for an airplane in a crowded, noisy, depressing airport far from home?

Then there are technical limits to wireless devices. Will hordes of customers keep signing up for gizmos whose displays are so much smaller than PC screens? Will the wizards in white lab coats improve the connections so they're as reliable as ground-line phones? Can the software techies beef up the programs so they can handle more complex research reports, stock charts, and asset-allocation models? And what can be done about those itsy-bitsy keypads that so many people find hard to use?

These are some of the reasons many professional investors see the growth of wireless slowing. "The sector has held up well," says MAXfunds.com's Burr. "But I don't expect it to be long before the hot hand of wireless of will settle into more of a traditional rate of return."

So feel free to bet on wireless. Just be prepared to watch the sector closely and fold your hand if it starts to cool.

SPOTTING WINNERS FOR THE LONG HAUL

The Internet is like the railroad industry. Only instead of hauling people and cargo, it carries data.

Now ask yourself this: After the railroad is built, after the basic network of tracks is laid, who stands to make the most money from it? Is it railroad companies themselves, or businesses that suddenly benefit from this new way to get parts and supplies and then move their finished products to market?

When it comes to the Internet, in the long run investment professionals aren't betting on infrastructure companies. The smart money is on businesses whose creative spirit will find a multitude of ways to cut costs and boost profits, using this new method for moving information.

Ironically, perhaps, those are mostly conventional businesses born well before the Internet. They don't have dot-com names. What they do have are visions for how they can turbocharge their existing revenues and profits by making use of the Net.

"When you ask what sort of investments will pan out over the next five years rather than in the short haul, my answer is to look at new-economy businesses," says Burr.

Kinetics Asset Management's Doyle agrees. "I personally believe that over an extended period, it will be 'new paradigm' investments that win," Doyle says. "These are already established companies that have incredible returns on equity. Their existing returns are predictable looking into the future. Whatever they can add by using the Internet is a plus."

In other words, the winners will be strong companies that are already leaders in their fields. They will find new ways to remain leaders, and possibly to push into new industries where they can be leaders as well.

It will be a case of the rich getting richer.

Paul Cook, manager of Munder NetNet Fund, one of the original net-fund quartet, says that TMP Worldwide is an example of a New Economy stock. The company was created in 1967 as Telephone Marketing Products, an enterprise devoted to selling advertising in the Yellow Pages. It has since grown into the world's largest Yellow-Pages advertising agency. And it has expanded its lines of business. It is also now a leading executive-search firm. Plus, in 1995 it acquired Monster.com, which is the top job-search web site.

"This is the type of offline play our fund likes," says Cook. "They have a traditional business plan, but they recognize the digital opportunities of the Internet. They've started to leverage that as a strategic tool to take market share from their traditional opponents."

Cook adds, "TMP Worldwide runs the Monster Board. If you're an information-technology professional looking to become some company's chief information officer, you look at the Monster Board to see what opportunities are out there. If you're a company looking for someone to run your IT infrastructure, you might list an opening for a CIO. They are the eBay of human-placement services."

This business plan has paid off. "About one-third of their revenues are now from on-line activities. But nearly the majority of their profits are from those on-line activities because they're more profitable. And most of their growth is from on-line businesses."

TMP Worldwide says 480 of the Fortune 500 companies are its clients.

Cook summarizes how he sees prospects for New Economy investments: "We think the Internet's reach is broad and is expanding. Eventually, it will reach into perhaps every sector of the economy. Five years from now my portfolio may look more like the S&P 500 than like a tech sector fund. That's because it will be big, successful, traditional companies that take advantage the most of the Internet."

TREACHEROUS CURRENTS

Even once you start to recognize funds by their strategies, choosing a good one isn't as simple as painting by numbers. For one thing, no matter which segment of the Net is hot at any moment, individual companies within the segment don't all perform alike. And even if companies within a segment did march in lockstep, not all funds plying that category invest in the same stocks at the same moment in the same amounts. At the very least, funds end up with similar baskets of stocks, but their costs differ either slightly or a lot. Over time those differences add up, and that's part of why funds with identical strategies can end up with very different investment returns.

But the main reason choosing a fund by its strategy isn't simple is because there's no such thing as a strategy that works better than others all the time. Some strategies fare better in certain market conditions than others. And the market doesn't stay the same. Like a river, its course can meander. Its flow can be placid for long stretches, then it can race through treacherous rapids and waterfalls.

Many of those rapids and twists and turns can be caused by boulders beneath the surface. You can't see them, but their effects are big. And those changes can be disastrous for some investors, advantageous for others. Underwater boulders can tear the bottom out of swift but fragile canoes. Slow flat-bottom boats may float above danger without suffering harm.

When it comes to mutual funds, the ever-changing market can make it harder to compare one fund with another. When one fund starts to outperform another, you have to ask whether it's because of something the fund is doing. Or is it because of the market? And will a fund's success continue next month or next year, when the market is flowing differently again?

The market hit rapids *and* waterfalls in the spring and early summer of 2000. Instead of the smooth climb upward they had enjoyed in previous years, Net funds had to cope for the first time with a wobbly market. This seesawing stock market was historically normal. The uninterrupted joy-ride straight up—especially in 1999—was the real exception to the rule.

That shift in conditions forced investors to ask themselves a question: Is it better to be in a swift but fragile canoe? or a sluggish flat-bottom boat?

The answer: It all depends where you are—which river, which part.

Chapter 11

How the Pros Invest in the Net

A hungry lion has an appetite for red meat. Likewise, any reader of this book wants to know how highly accomplished professional Internet investors put their money to work.

We'll take a look at how some Internet fund managers invest. In fact, let's dissect two funds that behaved very differently over the course of one year. By contrasting their strategies, we'll get a better idea of how each was pursuing success. It will also put into sharper focus what worked and what went wrong.

Table 11.1 shows the performance of Internet funds during the 12 months ending August 10, 2000, a randomly selected period of time. For perspective, performance during the second quarter of 2000 is also shown. As you can see, many of these quickly proliferating funds did not exist for the entire trailing year.

Although all of these funds invest in the same industrial sector—the Internet—they achieved very different results. There was a gap of more than 64 percentage points between the best- and worst-performing funds during the 12 months. ING Internet Fund (A class shares) racked up a return of 93.22 percent. Bringing up the rear was

Table 11.1 Performance by Selected Internet Funds for Twelve Months

			Return (percent)	
			2nd Qtr 2000	*1 Year*
Fund Family and Fund Name	*Size (in $ millions)*	*Starting Date*	*3/31/00–6/30/00*	*12 Months Ending 8/10/00*
Amerindo Technology (A)	23.0	8/7/98	–26.7	28.18
Amerindo Technology (D)	442.0	10/28/96	–26.69	28.45
Analysts Internet	2.1	5/4/99	–15.52	34.96
Enterprise Internet (A)	167.5	7/1/99	–21.69	74.88
Enterprise Internet (B)	172.7	7/1/99	–21.74	73.58
Enterprise Internet (C)	58.2	7/1/99	–21.8	73.39
Enterprise Internet (Y)	1.0	7/1/99	–21.6	75.19
Firsthand e-Commerce	501.5	9/30/99	–5.475	N/A
Goldman Sachs Internet Tollkeeper (A)	1050.0	10/1/99	–8.91	N/A
Goldman Sachs Internet Tollkeeper (B)	960.0	10/1/99	–9.09	N/A
Goldman Sachs Internet Tollkeeper (C)	551.0	10/1/99	–9.1	N/A
Goldman Sachs Internet Tollkeeper (I)	158.0	10/1/99	–8.74	N/A
Goldman Sachs Internet Tollkeeper (Svc)	N/A	10/1/99	–8.92	N/A
Investec internet.com	38.5	7/30/99	–22.53	64.51
ING Internet (A)	83.0	7/1/99	–26.34	93.22
ING Internet (B)	50.0	7/1/99	–26.49	92.22

ING Internet (C)	25.0	7/1/99	–26.51	92.1
ING Internet (X)	5.0	7/1/99	–26.41	N/A
Jacob Internet	116.2	12/13/99	–36.76	N/A
Kinetics Internet	819.3	10/21/96	–33.42	33.78
Kinetics Internet Emerging Growth	9.4	12/31/99	–34.45	N/A
Kinetics Internet Global Growth	19.6	12/31/99	–21.54	N/A
Kinetics Internet Infrastructure	17.8	12/31/99	–27.15	N/A
Kinetics Internet New Paradigm	3.1	12/31/99	–12.55	N/A
Mercury Internet Strategies (A)	0.1	3/22/00	–17.9	N/A
Mercury Internet Strategies (B)	0.1	3/22/00	–18.12	N/A
Mercury Internet Strategies (C)	0.1	3/22/00	–18.12	N/A
Mercury Internet Strategies (I)	0.1	3/22/00	–17.79	N/A
Merrill Lynch Internet Strategies (A)	141.6	3/20/00	–17.67	N/A
Merrill Lynch Internet Strategies (B)	383.7	3/20/00	–18.01	N/A
Merrill Lynch Internet Strategies (C)	225.0	3/20/00	–18.01	N/A
Merrill Lynch Internet Strategies (D)	94.1	3/20/00	–17.79	N/A
Monument Digital Technology (A)	113.4	11/3/98	–21.67	68.17
Monument Digital Technology (B)	23.9	10/4/99	–21.78	N/A

(Continued)

Table 11.1 Continued

Fund Family and Fund Name	*Size (in $ millions)*	*Starting Date*	*Return (percent)* 2nd Qtr 2000 3/31/00–6/30/00	*Return (percent)* 1 Year 12 Months Ending 8/10/00
Munder NetNet (A)	2911.4	8/19/96	–19.25	81.64
Munder NetNet (B)	3323.8	6/1/98	–19.4	80.29
Munder NetNet (C)	1661.2	6/1/98	–19.4	80.3
Munder NetNet (Y)	27.3	6/1/98	–19.21	82.02
RS Internet Age	211.8	12/1/99	–16.01	N/A
Rydex Internet (Adv)	65.6	4/3/00	N/A	N/A
Rydex Internet (Inv)	7.0	4/3/00	N/A	N/A
StockJungle Pure Play	0.7	11/17/99	–25.5	N/A
Strong Internet Fund	89.4	12/31/99	–15.27	N/A
Unified Select Internet	2.4	4/7/99	–26.73	49.56
WWW Internet Fund	N/A	8/1/96	–17.48	65.11

This table shows how selected Internet funds performed during the 12 months ended on August 10, 2000, and during the second quarter of 2000. Even though these funds all invest in the same industrial sector—the Internet—they achieved very different results. The best-performing fund during the 12 months was ING Internet Fund (A class shares), which gained 93.22 percent. The caboose was Amerindo Technology (D class shares), which advanced only 28.45 percent.

"N/A" means not available.

Source: Lipper.

Amerindo Technology Fund (D class shares), which gained only 28.45 percent.

But don't dismiss Amerindo Tech as some chronic laggard. It's anything but. The fund is run by Alberto Vilar and Gary Tanaka, two of the fund world's pioneers of Internet investing. Over time, this duo has run up such impressive investment scores that their fund's average annual return for the past three years is more than 68 percent. That's more than sixfold better than the typical stock fund does yearly. Not surprisingly, only four funds that invest in American companies have outdone Amerindo Tech.

So if the fund is making no more headway than a man trying to run up the side of a steep sand dune, it's not because the fund managers don't know their business. Vilar and Tanaka definitely know how to pick high-tech stocks.

What, then, explains the difference between Amerindo Tech's one-year track record and ING Internet's? Why did one of these Wall Street gladiators outpoint the other by so much?

To borrow a phrase from sports, let's start with the tale of the tape.

THE WEIGH-IN

Like professional boxers, funds often shape up differently. In this matchup between Amerindo Tech (which we think of as one of the wily old champs of Internet investing) and ING Internet (the upstart challenger), the differences are big. Amerindo Tech, which opened October 28, 1996, managed a combined $465 million in shareholder money as Table 11.1 shows. ING Internet's various share classes, which began July 1, 1999, held only $163 million.

The image flip-flops when the funds' corporate parents are compared. ING Investment Management, a Dutch company whose U.S. operations are based in Atlanta, handles $190 billion for investors. Amerindo Investment Advisors, which is headquartered in San Francisco but whose name reflects its multinational roots, runs $5.8 billion worth of investments.

And why does that matter? After all, bragging about "My dad is bigger than your dad" doesn't count for much except in a fourth-grade playground argument. But a big corporate parent can be helpful.

A parent company, known as an *investment advisor*, can provide behind-the-scenes help such as researchers and analysts. So a mutual fund with a large investment advisor behind it is like a boxer with an extra trainer or cut man in his corner. If the trainer or cut man knows his stuff, it's a potential edge.

At the fund level, ING Internet has a single manager. That's a contrast to Amerindo's tandem brain trust. But like his counterparts at Amerindo, Guy Uding has been at ING Internet's helm since it opened for business.

RING STRATEGY

So much for the prelim. The main event consists of each fund's investments. If you want to understand why these funds have different records at any given time, look at where they've put their money to work.

Look at each one's investment strategies. There are important differences. Not all boxers are alike. Some like to stand toe-to-toe with an opponent and slug it out. Others like to jab and dance around the ring, tiring an opponent and avoiding his punches. So too funds have different approaches to winning.

While Amerindo happens to specialize in Internet investing, officially its objective is to invest in technology companies. The fund's prospectus specifies that. The entire world of technology is of course much wider than the Internet segment. The prospectus tells people considering investing in the fund that it will fish for investments in the Internet as well as in high-tech industries that may or may not involve the Net, such as computers. It will even cast its net among companies that make medical devices and in the realm of biotechnology.

ING, on the other hand, is all Internet, all the time. In boxing jargon, it is a straight-ahead Net fund.

One area where the funds are similar is in the size of companies they invest in. Amerindo's holdings average about $10.1 billion in market value. Companies like that are generally considered medium-size, although they're on the threshold of being categorized as large. ING's companies are about $9.7 billion in size.

One way the two funds more clearly differ is in the size of their respective portfolios. Amerindo invests in fewer companies. That's known as being more *concentrated*. The fund holds only 22 stocks as of its latest portfolio disclosure date. ING is not a giant fund either. It has only 38 stocks. Some mutual funds hold 300, 400, or more stocks. So ING Internet's portfolio may not sound much bigger than Amerindo Tech's portfolio. But it's enough to let ING do one thing that Amerindo can't: hedge its bets.

By focusing on so few stocks, Amerindo's investments get magnified. If its best investment ideas work well, the fund's performance looks great. There are few other stocks in its portfolio to dilute gains made by its big winners. But this is a live-by-the-sword, die-by-the-sword strategy. If just a few stocks have a bad month, bad quarter, or bad year—watch out! There aren't enough other stocks in the portfolio to offset those.

It's like the boxer who comes out swinging and going for a knockout right away. If he lands solid punches, he wins. But if he hasn't turned out his opponent's lights by, say, the fifth round, he's liable to punch himself out. Fatigue sets in. He's vulnerable.

Something like that is what happened during the year 2000.

LACING UP THE GLOVES

Now compare the fund's actual investments. This is an imprecise science because the information is rarely up-to-the-moment. Only a small number of mutual funds tell shareholders what's in the portfolio right now. This book's analysis uses the latest information disclosed by the funds. But neither posts their current holdings. (Funds are secretive because they don't want their competitors to know what they are buying and selling. They don't want to give away good investment ideas to those competitors. And they don't want to drive up the price of a stock they're buying by broadcasting their interest in it.)

So when we examine each fund's holdings, we know we're looking at stocks they owned during the 12 months under discussion. But we don't know which holdings might have changed by the end of the period.

Still, the fact that the funds held these stocks during this period gives us a snapshot of what the fund managers were trying to accomplish. Better yet, that snapshot was taken while the stock market downturn for Internet stocks was about two months underway.

That's the key. Take our hypothetical boxer again. If you want to know why he gets knocked down, for example, you've got to look at where his hands were before and during his opponent's punches. Ditto for his foot-work. How exposed was his chin? What was he doing in the moments leading up to getting clobbered? Whether he gets up off the canvas and what he does next is another story. That's about what comes later.

So knowing which stocks these funds held when market trouble started (in March 2000) is all that matters for this analysis. It shows us why each fund suffered differently.

How the funds coped with the falling market once it was already underway is a different issue. *That* will shed light on how well each fund rebounded.

BLOW-BY-BLOW ACCOUNT

Let's look first at the big picture. In terms of categories, ING Internet reports that a whopping 59.7 percent of its money was invested in Internet software firms as of early summer, well after the tech-sector meltdown had begun in March. Many of those are further categorized as infrastructure stocks, because they *enable* other companies to use the Internet. On the other hand, only 4.5 percent of its money was at work in e-commerce companies.

How about Amerindo? Only 35.8 percent of the fund's holdings fell into the Internet software category. In contrast, 22.9 percent were e-commerce stocks. And e-commerce stocks were one of the hardest-hit Internet categories during that market tumble. Meanwhile, infrastructure stocks of all kinds fared far better.

Now take a look at each fund's biggest investments. Table 11.2 shows how ING Internet's five biggest holdings fared in the 12 months ended September 7, 2000. ING Internet had one knockout stock, TIBCO Software. The Palo Alto, California-based company gained nearly 800 percent during the 12-month period.

TIBCO's software helps companies do business over the Web. It does that by enabling companies to integrate regular backroom and point-of-sale systems with e-commerce systems such as online marketplaces and exchanges. And it weaves all of those software systems together in real time, as events are actually happening.

The fact that this firm fared better than many e-commerce companies in its customer pool starkly illustrates what the stock market did in early 2000. It began to punish e-commerce companies that didn't have sufficient revenues and earnings. But TIBCO was making money by selling services *to* e-commerce enterprises. The marketplace judged that the stock did not deserve a trip to Wall Street's woodshed.

The second-best performer in its top-five holdings was Broadcom. Like virtually every tech stock, this company's shares got trounced in the spring of 2000. Its share price lost more than half its value in only three weeks, falling from a March 23 peak of $253. But it rocketed back from that setback. Even *with* that interruption, the stock climbed 267 percent in the 12 months ended September 7, 2000.

The reason Wall Street loved this Irvine, California-based company

Table 11.2 ING Internet Fund's Ten Biggest Holdings

Name of Stock	*Percent of Fund Assets Invested*	*Share-Price Change*
Software.com, Inc.	5.6%	246.7%
VeriSign, Inc.	5.3%	218.4%
TIBCO Software, Inc.	5.1%	796.8%
Broadcom Corp.	4.4%	267.0%
Yahoo! Inc.	4.3%	38.0%
Cisco Systems, Inc.	4.1%	
America Online, Inc.	4.0%	
BroadVision, Inc.	3.9%	
Critical Path, Inc.	3.8%	
Inktomi Corp.	3.7%	
Total invested in top 10:	44.2%	

These were ING Internet Fund's 10 largest investments as of June 30, 2000. The right column shows how much the five biggest holdings' share prices grew in value in the 12 months ended September 7, 2000.
Sources: ING Investment Management, *Investor's Business Daily.*

is that it is the developer of the computer chips behind many high-speed broadband technologies. Whether you get online through a cable modem, a DSL connection, or a high-speed office network, you're probably using a device that contains a Broadcom integrated circuit.

That's market leadership, big time. And that's an example of why investors loved infrastructure companies.

The third-best performer in the company's top five was Software.com. It gained about 247 percent in the year we're looking at. Also, this stock was the fund's largest holding. It had 5.6 percent of its money invested in the company. That magnified the stock gain's boost to the fund's overall performance.

This firm fits the software infrastructure category because its programs let Internet service providers play *Post Office*. Its product by that name (as well as another program called *InterMail*) runs e-mail and messaging systems for ISPs and their customers. Its programs also give ISPs the ability to offer web-based fax service. Its clients include Ma Bell, Baby Bells like Ameritech, Time Warner, and Internet portals like Excite@Home.

Currently, it is being taken over by Phone.com, whose products help make possible the delivery of Internet data to mobile telephones. That makes it a key player in the emergence of wireless Internet access.

ING Internet's fourth-strongest stock among its top five was VeriSign. The company, based in Mountain View, California, more than doubled in price, gaining better than 218 percent.

VeriSign's software stamps digital codes onto data transmissions and transactions conducted on the Net, verifying the identity of the sender. The confirmation code is like a notary public's stamp on a printed document, certifying the authenticity of someone's signature. Companies like American Express, Microsoft, and Visa have used VeriSign software for online activities that include e-mail, home banking, and credit-card purchases.

Rounding out ING Internet's top five was Yahoo!, which gained 38 percent. Next to the other top holdings, Yahoo! sounds like it had a bad year. But a 38 percent advance is actually excellent compared with the 10 percent growth a year that all stocks average.

Yahoo! is the top-drawing Internet portal, drawing nearly 50 million visitors each month. In turn, those eyeballs lure more than 5,000 advertisers. That gives this Santa Clara, California-based company modest but rapidly growing profits—a boast most dot-coms can only dream about.

Now, how did Amerindo Tech's top holdings compare?

"IN THE FAR CORNER . . ."

When you pit each fund's largest investments against each other, the battle between each pair of stocks is comparable to a round in our boxing match.

Round one: each fund's top performer. In the period we're looking at, the best of ING's five largest investments was TIBCO Software, with a gain exceeding 796 percent. As Table 11.3 shows, the best of Amerindo's biggest holdings was Ariba, which techies and investment bankers describe as a maker of enabling software. In plain English, what this company does is create software that helps companies use the Web to buy and sell goods and services.

Its market is the backroom world of procurement departments in

Table 11.3 Amerindo Technology Fund's Ten Biggest Holdings

Name of Stock	*Share-Price Change*
Ariba, Inc.	345.5%
Inktomi Corp.	109.2%
eBay, Inc.	–50.2%
Yahoo! Inc.	38.0%
Protein Design Labs, Inc.	215.4%
Broadcom Corp.	
OnDisplay, Inc.	
Gilead Sciences, Inc.	
CMGI, Inc.	
Homestore.com, Inc.	
Total invested in top 10:	**64.22%**

Amerindo Technology Fund had 64.22 percent of its money invested in its 10 largest holdings as of June 30, 2000. This shows how much the fund's five biggest investments grew or fell in share prices in the 12 months ended September 7, 2000.

Sources: Amerindo Investment Advisors, *Investor's Business Daily.*

big corporations. Its customers are the men and women who buy everything from new desks for their companies' bean counters to paper towels for the rest rooms. They use Ariba software to wheel and deal either directly with suppliers or through online auctions.

The Mountain View, California company currently has the biggest slice of that *e-procurement business*. That makes it—here come some Wall Street buzzwords—a *market leader* in its industry. Investors like market leaders because they tend to be the most profitable companies in their field, the biggest, and the most likely to survive. Also, their size and profits enable them to kick sand in the face of smaller competitors.

So Ariba was a perfectly reasonable investment for Amerindo Tech. In fact, it was the fund's largest investment. And its performance was excellent. Just not as outstanding as TIBCO Software's. Its gain was less than half TIBCO's.

Round two: Amerindo Tech's second-best top holding was Protein Design Labs. This company's stock gained about 215 percent in the 12 months we're examining. That's a very good year. But like Ariba, its performance was not as good as its counterpart at ING.

Although this was the fund's fifth-largest investment, for better or worse the company isn't even an Internet stock. The firm develops antibodies and other drugs that battle viral infections, autoimmune diseases, and certain cancers. Still, the technology underlying the company's research involves the same types of computers and microchips that have such a huge impact on the Internet. We'll discuss more about this later in this chapter.

Round three: Amerindo's third-best stock among its top five was Inktomi. Another California company (this one is based in Foster City), Inktomi is best known for search-engine and directory software used by portals like America Online. It also makes programs that let people do online comparison shopping. Also, it's been pushing into the market for software that speeds up audio and video broadcasts on the Net. It advanced about 109 percent in our time period. Nice; in fact, *very* nice. But less than half as good as ING's third-best stock.

Round four: Amerindo's fourth-best big stock was Yahoo!. The portal, which gained 38 percent, was ING's fifth-best holding.

Round five: Completing the fund's top five was eBay, the online auction hall. This cyberforum gets its income from listing and selling fees, and is growing rapidly. It is expanding into business-to-business auctions, for example, and into more countries. It has established itself as one of the leaders in its—here's another dose of Wall Street lexicon—*space*.

One big problem, though, is that its yearly profits are measured in pennies. The profits on one share of stock (not that it's common for anyone to own a single share) won't even buy a pack of Twinkies.

Another problem is at least partially a matter of perception. The company is in the segment of the Internet that investors hammered so hard during 2000—the business-to-consumer sector. As a result, the company's stock was clobbered during the period we're looking at. It fell more than 50 percent. Meanwhile, ING Internet's third-largest stock was the red-hot TIBCO.

Compounding the soft stock's impact on Amerindo Tech was its size. It was the fund's third-biggest holding. The fund declines to disclose the size of individual investments, but the web site run by Morningstar, a fund-research firm, pegs the stock's weighting as of the end of 1999 as 7.4 percent of the portfolio. Taking up that much of Amerindo's money, the stock's drop would drag the fund down like an anchor.

MOMENT OF TRUTH

So it turns out that Amerindo Tech's heavyweight holdings got outscored in each round. That pulls into sharper focus the fund's trailing performance in the period we're looking at. The bigger, older fund didn't lose the fight due to mysterious causes that are clear only to some high priests of Wall Street voodoo. The explanation makes sense to ordinary residents of Main Street, U.S.A. It's right there in plain sight for anyone who knows where to look, which is what *Getting Started in Internet Investing* teaches you.

The fund lost because its investments didn't perform as well as the other fund's. Stock-by-stock among the top five, ING's grew more in value. The fund's own share price did the same thing, as faithfully as a chick following its mother goose.

Among those five-biggest bets by each fund, Amerindo's best didn't even do half as well as ING's. One of Amerindo's stocks suffered a 50 percent decline during the 12 months. None of ING's top holdings slid at all. And the simple arithmetic average (which is what we have to settle for; we can't do a true average that would reflect the dollar weighting of each stock because Amerindo does not reveal the size of individual holdings) share-price gain for ING's top stocks was a shade higher than 313 percent. That's almost two-and-a-half times better than Amerindo Tech's.

And the reason the funds made different investments is that each was pursuing a different strategy. Amerindo held fewer investments, making it more aggressive as an investor. It put all of its eggs into fewer baskets. But ING Internet put its money to work in stocks that were more productive.

Amerindo Tech was like a deadly brawler, trying to score a knockout with a few big blows. But ING Internet was a boxer, preferring to dance around the ring and score points with its jab. Its carefully aimed punches took a cumulative toll, winning this particular bout.

Fish or Fowl?

An additional point about Amerindo Technology Fund's orientation: One reason Amerindo Tech is viewed as an Internet fund despite the broad stock-hunting ground it lays claim to in its prospectus is that much of its portfolio happens to consist of Internet stocks. Another reason is the general technology, medical-device, and biotechnology companies in which it also invests use the same emerging technologies that make the Internet such an exciting industry. In other words, it's the same companies supplying the underlying technologies in computers, computer chips, and software.

"The Internet is much more than a collection of dot-com companies," says Robert Markman, head of the Markman MultiFunds. "It is everything involved with electronic technology. Any business whose technology depends on the movement of electrons is tied to the Internet, directly or indirectly. When I talk about investing in the Internet, I'm talking about investing in the broad range of electronic and knowledge-based industries."

Markman MultiFunds has no Internet funds per se. But about 80 percent of its stock holdings are in technology companies.

"Most people think of biotech as a field filled with guys working in labs, surrounded by beakers and test tubes," Markman says. "But the advances we're seeing in biotechnology are due to advances in computers. The guys in the labs are figuring out things with computers that are now able to run series of deep computations. That increased computer speed is due to companies making faster chips. And those same chips can run fiber-optic lasers, routers, servers—the infrastructure of the Internet.

"Amerindo Tech Fund has always been investing in the cutting edge of those technologies. Sometimes it looks like they're investing way out in left field. But few people have been as right about the directions being taken by new technologies. *That's* why Amerindo Tech is an Internet fund."

Chapter 12

Shotgun versus Sharpshooting Approach

One thing you learned in Chapter 11 was that by aiming at different segments of the Internet industry, two funds performed very differently over the course of 12 months. ING Internet Fund bought stocks in companies that were much more profitable than Amerindo Technology Fund's. As a result, shares owned by ING Internet rose a lot more than Amerindo's. Over those 12 months, ING Internet's own share price rose, riding on the backs of its holdings.

So profits are the name of the game. The concept is clear. And companies' profits are easy enough to see in hindsight. But how do you predict them in advance? You can't, not with 100 percent certainty anyway. But you can improve your odds. One way to do that is by aiming at as large a target as possible.

Make no mistake, you're not *required* to do that. If you are among the readers of *Getting Started in Internet Investing* who are the most willing to take on calculated investment risks, you may choose to do the opposite. You can aim at a small target. That's what you'd be doing when you invest in a mutual fund that targets companies that are similar to each other. If stock in all of them goes up at the same time, your fund's shares skyrocket in value. *Bingo*!

But that doesn't give you much margin for error. If the market does not do exactly what you expect, your fund isn't holding other investments that can act as life preservers, keeping its share price buoyant.

The solution is to aim at more than one type of company at a time. That's *diversification*. Chances are not all of them will hit the jackpot. You won't do as well as you would by having bet only on the one or two types that do hit the jackpot. But you'd still do well, and you'd protect yourself from having bet *only* on the types of companies that don't do well.

So by diversifying you sacrifice some potential gain. But you build in protection and increase your odds of being at least partially correct.

If you don't expect to be the next Dead-eye Dick of Internet investing, then aiming for a broader, more diverse target is the safer strategy. It's the same reason a lot of sheriffs in the old Wild West toted a shotgun for protection. They didn't have to be a sharpshooter. All they had to do was point it in the right general direction, and pull the trigger.

AIMING AT DIFFERENT TARGETS

Let's compare two funds. Their performances were polar opposites. As Table 12.1 shows, Strong Internet Fund was the strongest Internet fund through the first eight-months-plus of 2000.

On average, Internet funds lost nearly 20 percent in that period. But Strong Internet was down less than 3 percent. Meanwhile, the laggard among Net funds in that time was Jacob Internet, which had lost more than 53 percent of its value. For every $100 you had invested with that fund on January 1, by August 10 you could take out only $46.93.

What were those two funds doing differently? The most obvious difference was that they were investing in different types of companies. In fact, Jacob Internet Fund focused largely on one segment of the Internet. Early in the year, a large portion of its money was invested in

Table 12.1 Fund Performance Comparison: Jacob Internet versus Strong Internet

Fund	*2000 Performance (through Aug. 10)*
Jacob Internet	–53.07
Strong Internet	–2.9
Average for 45 Internet funds	–19.07
S&P 500 Index	0.094

During the first 223 days of 2000, a dramatic investment-return gap opened between the top-performing Internet fund and the laggard in that period. In fact, for every $1,000 you had invested in Strong Internet at the first of the year, by August 10 it had shrunk to $971. But only $469.30 of your $1,000 would be left in Jacob Internet. Different investments by each fund explained how two funds investing in the same general field could post such contrasting results.
Source: Lipper.

the stocks of consumer-oriented companies. Broadly speaking, these were business-to-consumer (B2C) stocks. More specifically, they were companies that provide content or operate tools for finding or using content.

Look at some of them. Ask Jeeves is what's called a *search-engine company*. The firm's software is a sort of high-tech butler that fetches what you request on the Internet, responding to plain English inquiries rather than disembodied key words or, in techie lingo, *Boolean logic* commands. iVillage runs web sites aimed at women. About.com provides a content-and-search service. Priceline.com runs a name-your-own-price shopping service.

Through the first nine months of 2000, each one's stock had lost between about 50 percent and 80 percent of its value. Sound familiar? Jacob Internet Fund lost more than 50 percent in that period.

In contrast, Strong Internet Fund had big investments in such companies as Broadcom and Cisco Systems. Broadcom is the developer of ubiquitous computer chips that are the brains running many high-speed communications gizmos, from modems to DSL connections and cable-TV set-top boxes. Cisco is the dominant maker of routers, those computers that rule the Internet. That's akin to owning a monopoly on the manufacture of traffic signal devices in the United States.

Over the first nine months of that year, Cisco's stock gained 3.2 percent. That may not sound like much, but would you rather have that gain or the precipitous losses of Jacob Internet's consumer-focused stocks? Better yet, Broadcom's stock grew about 84 percent.

DIVERSITY AMONG LINES OF BUSINESS

But simply aiming at different targets alone does not make one fund better diversified. That just means Jacob Internet Fund had its money in the wrong place at the wrong time. Strong Internet Fund was more diversified in part because it had spread its eggs among more baskets.

Check out its portfolio. As Table 12.2 shows, right before the market's big selloff of technology and Internet stocks in spring 2000, Jacob Internet Fund had huge portions of its money invested in segments of

Table 12.2 Jacob Internet's Investments

Business Sector	*Portion of Fund's Money Invested*
Internet content	52.6%
Internet retail e-commerce	19.9%
Internet software	19.2%
Internet finance	4.7%
Advertising	2.2%
Retail catalog	1.8%

Shortly before the content, electronic commerce, and advertising sectors suffered some of the worst losses by Internet business sectors during the spring of 2000, Jacob Internet Fund was top-heavy with them.
Source: Jacob Asset Management.

the Internet that were about to tumble farthest. It had a staggering 52.6 percent of its money invested in Internet content companies. The fund had another 19.9 percent tied up in e-tailers, those B2C companies that had been so hot before spring 2000. That's almost three-quarters of its money invested in sectors that cooled the most.

In comparison, Strong Internet Fund had a modest 10.7 percent in the content sector. Overall, its money was spread much more evenly around the Internet. Table 12.3 shows how six business segments held similar portions of the fund's money. They were within four percentage points of each other in size. In fact, Strong's biggest and smallest segments differed by only 11.3 percentage points. Jacob's biggest and smallest segments were more than 50 percentage points apart in size.

Table 12.3 Strong Internet's Investments

Business Sector	*Portion of Fund's Money Invested*
Internet network security	14.7%
Internet software	13.2%
Telecommunications equipment	12.1%
Electronics/semiconductor manufacturing	11.9%
Computers/local networks	11.2%
Internet service providers/content	10.7%
Enterprise software	8.5%
Telecommunications services	5.1%
Computer manufacturers	4.6%
E-commerce	3.4%

Strong Internet Fund had its money invested much more evenly around Internet business segments.
Note: Funds do not necessarily use identical terminology in describing business segments. Data as of July 31, 2000.
Source: Strong Investments.

DIVERSITY BY COMPANY SIZE

Having too many eggs in a single basket was one problem for Jacob Internet Fund. Not spreading risk in terms of the sizes of companies it invested in was a second problem.

While Jacob Internet was fishing for smaller companies that could grow rapidly—if they lived long enough—Strong Internet was investing in the stocks of bigger, more mature companies. On its Web site, the fund declares that its strategy is to invest in companies of all sizes. Having done that, when the Internet market went south Strong Internet had more of its money bet on better-established corporations. With their steadier revenues, they were better able to generate profits that buoyed their share prices.

While Jacob Internet was hunting for geese (ones that could lay golden eggs), Strong Internet had its sights set on bigger game. The typical company in Strong Internet's portfolio was $25.9 billion in market size. That's different from size in terms of sales. Market size or capitalization is measured by multiplying the company's stock price by the number of shares. It's a standard way of comparing corporate dimensions and capacity. To put that into perspective with a household name (which was not in Strong's portfolio), oil-company Texaco had a market cap of $27.6 billion at that time, with yearly sales of $43.5 billion.

In contrast, Jacob Internet's typical stock was only $1 billion to $2 billion big. That's the size range of A.C. Nielsen (not owned by the fund), which measures TV audiences. That firm was $1.4 billion in size, with yearly revenues of $1.5 billion.

"We invest in young companies that are early in their business life cycle," said fund manager Ryan Jacob.

A market size of $1 billion and $2 billion may sound like a lot of money compared with your household budget, but it's lilliputian in the brobdignagian world of Corporate America.

Companies that small don't have a lot of extra cash in the bank to see them through rough spots—and the market was very rough during 2000. They don't have mammoth advertising budgets to fight for market share and sales. They can't afford to do all of the market research they'd like to or even hire the very best executives. And they don't have the sheer girth to avoid being swallowed like a piece of candy by some predatory company.

"Some funds specialize in different business sectors of the Internet," said Cathy Baker, comanager of a third Net fund, RS Internet Fund, about her industry in general. "Some of the biggest differences among Internet funds have to do with size of companies they invest in."

FOCUSED ON CURRENT PROFITS

Jacob's game plan was to invest in young companies that have a lot of room to grow before they settle into maturity. When their growth spurt finally starts, their progress can be dramatic. And in early 2000 he was being patient. He had invested in companies whose growth explosion was not about to happen overnight.

"Companies like that are not being watched by a lot of investors. Their stock can be bought at very attractive prices," he said.

The numbers tell the story. Of Strong Internet's 10 biggest investments, eight were profitable in their latest fiscal year, as Table 12.4 shows. In Jacob Internet's case, detailed in Table 12.5, only a single one of its entire portfolio of 25 stocks had reported a profit in its most recent fiscal year.

It's certainly not that Jacob doesn't know how to spot winners. He is a pioneer of Internet investing, who has produced turbocharged performances. The fact is, his stellar returns have turned on many people to investing in the Net. As manager of Kinetics Internet Fund from December 20, 1997, through June 24, 1999, he steered the fund to a colossal gain topping 232 percent. That was more than tenfold better than what the overall market did.

If there were a hall of fame for Internet investing, that's the sort of run that would gain a portfolio manager a membership invitation.

No, Jacob Internet's problem was not a lack of stock-picking expertise. Its performance in 2000 was due to time frame. He was willing to wait longer for profitability among his holdings.

Table 12.4 Strong Internet's Profitable Investments

Stock	*Profit in Latest Fiscal Year?*
Broadcom	Yes
Cisco Systems	Yes
VeriSign	Yes
America Online	Yes
Jupiter Networks	No
Sun Microsystems	Yes
Sycamore Networks	Yes
Ariba	No
Check Point Software Technologies	Yes
E-Tek Dynamics	Yes

All but two of Strong Internet Fund's 10 largest investments as of July 31, 2000, were profitable in their most recent fiscal years.
Sources: Strong Internet Fund, *Investor's Business Daily.*

"I look for companies that are capable of growing into leadership positions within their fields," said Jacob. "But I don't demand that they reach leadership today. I'm willing to give them some time. I build a portfolio for the future."

Jacob knew what he was doing. This was a calculated strategy by a savvy professional. In the long run it may well pay off. But it illustrates another factor that you must take into consideration when deciding how to invest *your* money.

How long are you willing to wait for your investment to pay off? Do you want to plow all of your money into orchards whose trees won't bear fruit for a year or two—or longer? Or do you want your money spread among a variety of orchards, which will blossom one after another, providing you with an ongoing harvest cornucopia (not to mention protecting you from drought in any one year)?

Jacob's approach can pay off spectacularly. Remember, the fund he

Table 12.5 Jacob Internet's Profitable Investments

Stock	*Profit in Latest Fiscal Year?*
About.com	No
Aether Systems	No
Akamai	No
Ask Jeeves	No
Be Free	No
CMGI	No
Commerce One	No
Critical Path	No
Delias	No
Digital Insight	No
Doubleclick	No
Earthweb	No
eBay	Yes
GoTo.com	No
ITurf	No
iVillage	No
Keynote Systems	No
Lifeminders.com	No
Marketwatch.com	No
MyPoints.com	No
Netcentives	No
Phone.com	No
Priceline.com	No
724 Solutions	No
Starmedia Network	No

Only one stock in Jacob Internet Fund's entire portfolio as of July 31, 2000, had reported a profit in its most recent fiscal year.
Sources: Jacob Internet Fund, *Investor's Business Daily*.

ran in 1998 earned 196 percent. Compare that with how the overall market is doing this year—or any year.

But that technique requires patience, discipline, and courage. You must be willing to go through severe downturns in the *short run*—which may not seem so short while they drag on.

LEARN THE RIGHT LESSON

So Jacob Internet Fund invested in smaller companies. And during the first eight-months-plus of 2000, far fewer were profitable than Strong Internet Fund's holdings. And Jacob Internet did much worse than Strong Internet during that time.

But the size of the companies in Jacob Internet's portfolio does not explain why the fund didn't do as well as Strong Internet. Strong Internet Fund did better because, like a sheriff in the Wild West, it had a better chance of hitting its target—profitable companies—with a scatter gun, not a six-shooter.

With a broader investment approach, it spread its money among more businesses—51 versus 25. Strong Internet also put its money to work among more types of businesses. And it invested in companies of more sizes. Further, it focused on companies that were supposed to be more capable of churning out profits in the here and now.

Sure, a sharpshooter can get the glory. When a sharpshooter is on target, his or her performance is spectacular. But it's easier to get the job done with a shotgun approach. And the less time you can devote to playing Wall Street Big Shot, the better off you're likely to be in a fund that seeks more winners, rather than a fund that seeks a few very big winners.

All the information you require is easily obtainable, although all of it is unlikely to be in a single place. You can track down specifics about what stocks a fund owns in its:

- ✔ Prospectus
- ✔ Annual and semiannual reports

- ✔ Quarterly reports (if any)
- ✔ And at its web site

Among all of those, you will find lists of holdings, how much of each is owned, the percentage of a fund's money invested in each stock (or other security such as a bond), and how a fund's cash is spread among various business segments or industries. In periodic reports, the fund manager explains what went well and what didn't in the preceding period (typically six months or one business quarter).

Some funds provide more information and analysis than others. Some describe how a fund's investments and performance have changed recently. For other funds, you must compare the most recent holdings to holdings listed in previous reports to get a clearer picture of what's going on. Yes, it takes a little work, but placing two lists side-by-side and comparing them is not rocket science.

Outside sources, such as newspapers, magazines, and financial web sites, often explain things that funds themselves don't. And many of their web sites have search tools that let you look up information. You may need a pad of paper, pencil, and pocket calculator. Don't forget your stapler, and some file folders. But research is doable—and worth the effort.

We'll discuss where to find information and how to do research in more detail in Chapter 15.

Chapter 13

Ten-Step Investment Process

In Chapter 11, why did we compare mutual funds to pugilists rather than, say, factory robots?

Don't laugh. We could have. After all, if you go to any modern major car factory, you'll see robots hard at work on the assembly line. Okay, okay . . . *you* work hard, a robot just works. But even if that industrial cyborg doesn't sweat, get hungry, or need a coffee break, it does its job.

Day after day, it lifts and moves windshields, welds hinges to steel frames, and spits out paint. And except for the occasional breakdown, it does its job the same way over and over. Unless someone's fingers *tappety-tap* on a computer keyboard to change software commands, the robot works at the same speed, grabs parts with the same force, welds metals with the same amount of heat.

Wouldn't you like a mutual fund to be that reliably consistent? The trouble is that they can't be. First and foremost, they are run by humans, and they only do what their human managers call for. For another thing, they work on something that changes all the time. Unlike cars that roll off an assembly line identical to one another, each investment decision by a mutual fund involves stocks that vary from one another. And these decisions are made in the context of a constantly evolving marketplace and economy.

So mutual funds don't perform the same way day in, day out. And that's why you're not supposed to use this book as a tout sheet for specific stocks or funds. No one can tell you which stocks or funds to buy right now because the advice becomes dated. Tomorrow or next week or next month, the hot tip will have gone cold. The good ones aren't always good, and the rest aren't always losers.

The lesson of Chapter 11, where we compared two funds that performed differently during a random but interesting time period, is *not* that you must invest in ING Internet Fund. Nor are you supposed to avoid Amerindo Technology forever.

The value of Chapter 11 is in illustrating the process for finding winners. That way you can find what's poised to be hot whenever you happen to be on the prowl for an Internet investment. The process also takes into account not only what's poised to be hot, but what's appropriate for you. The process may point you toward Amerindo Tech at one time, ING Internet at another, or some other fund or stock.

Remember, the ranks of stocks and funds that are about to be winners can change from day to day. But the *process* for identifying those with the best prospects stays the same.

As we said: The good ones aren't always good, and the rest aren't always losers. The purpose of this book is to show you how to find the ones that are right for you.

"ON YOUR MARK, GET SET . . ."

Whether you are a polished veteran professional or a newcomer to Wall Street, successful investing requires you to take certain steps. As an individual investor, you can take comfort from the fact that these steps are the same for every investor, big or small, experienced or green. But not every investor executes these steps the same way, of course.

A professional money manager may have the luxury of resorting to sophisticated computer programs to identify companies that are attractive because their revenues and earnings are growing. You'll be able to do the same thing, whether you work only with a pad of paper and a pencil or a desktop computer that lets you massage a spreadsheet while surfing the web. You'll identify emerging sectors of the Internet, individual companies that are market leaders within those segments, and businesses with growing revenues and earnings—all of that, with information available in such sources as newspapers, at web sites, and through online screens that let you set criteria for your hunt. (More about those tools in Chapters 14 and 15.)

And individual investors just setting out aren't the only ones who must take care of basic steps like figuring out how much money they've got available to invest. In fact, institutional investors must keep careful track of how much cash on hand they've got. If they're forced to sell stocks to raise cash—either to pay off shareholders exiting their mutual fund, for example, or to buy an unexpected bargain—they risk incurring taxes. Shareholders hate that, and it reduces a fund's performance.

So while not every investor walks the same way, we've all got to cover the same ground. The process involves the following 10 steps. You've been introduced to several of them already. We'll deal with others in subsequent chapters. In any case, it's time to see how one leads to another so that you think of them as a *single process*.

Step 1: Identify Your Goals

Decide what your goals are as an investor. Let's call these your investment goals. How much money do you *need* to amass (notice we didn't ask how much you *want* to accumulate), and for what purposes? What are your priorities among those goals? If you can only pay for some of them, which are most important to you? If you can pay for some before others, which do you need sooner? Are there any that you can bear to give up on, if you don't reach your goals? Use Table 4.1 in Chapter 4 to make a list of your goals.

Step 2: Calculate an Overall Budget

What else do you need money for? What are your living expenses now? What will they be when you reach the deadline for each of those investment goals? Don't forget to count special expenses as well as regular ones. So include retirement nest egg targets, savings for junior's college degree (or your own!), paying for an offspring's wedding, buying a home, helping your own mom and dad with their retirement costs, and putting something aside for a rainy day fund (just in case some Internet firm runs your company into the ground). Use Table 4.2 to make a budget.

Step 3: Figure Out How Much You Can Invest

Okay, now how much money is left over? In other words, once you figure out how much you need to maintain your lifestyle, do you have anything left over to invest?

If not, you've got four choices: (1) cut spending; (2) get a raise; (3) revise your spending goals downward; (4) some combination of 1, 2, and 3. You can also try raising cash by picking pockets at a local mall. But we don't recommend it.

One way or another, though, you've got to get a handle on how much money is available for you to put to work. You'll see that on the bottom line at the end of Table 4.2.

Step 4: Determine How Large Your Bet on the Internet Should Be

Now that you've got a handle on how much money you can invest, you've got to decide how much of that to invest in the Internet.

Sounds easy. But since the Internet is one of Wall Street's most volatile neighborhoods, this decision starts with another choice: How much of your investment money do you want to expose to extreme risks? There's the risk of investments plunging in value overnight, the risk of money being tied up for long periods in investments that have shrunk in value, and the risk of outright loss—a forced separation from your money that you might refer to as, ahem, *cash-tration*.

The answer is different for everyone. It all depends on how much money you can spare for investments of any kind, your age, income, reliability of income, and circumstances. Make a decision about how much of that you can bear to lose for, say, two years in a row.

Determine your stomach for short-term gyrations and the long-term risk of your long green being reduced to short bread by taking our risk-tolerance quiz in Figure 5.1. Your answers to the quiz questions will help you decide whether you've got the stomach to invest in the Internet. If you can handle the ups and downs, the quiz will help you figure out how heavily to expose yourself to the Net—whether to make Internet investments a large, medium, or small part of your overall portfolio.

Step 5: Decide Whether to Invest in Stocks, Mutual Funds, or Both

All investors, including professionals, must decide how to deploy their financial resources. For you, that decision begins with deciding whether to do it through stocks, mutual funds, or both.

On the one hand, stocks give you more control over your investments. Mutual funds, in contrast, give you greater ease and safety.

By control, we mean that you get to target specific investments, without having some of your money spread over other investments as well, the way they are in a fund portfolio. Also, you alone decide when to sell or add shares of each stock you choose. And you don't get stuck with the tax baggage that accompanies shares in many mutual funds.

Control, though, comes at a price. To exercise your control, you've

Built-in Tax Burden

When you buy shares in a mutual fund, you join other shareholders in being liable for the fund's yearly tax bill. You're liable for your portion of the bill even if the fund triggered it before you became a shareholder. The bill stems from the fund's sale of stocks it owned. Shareholders—not the fund itself—owe tax on each profitable sale. That profit is known as a capital gain.

On the capital gain from securities the fund has owned more than a year, you're taxed at what's called the *long-term rate*. Usually, that's 20 percent. Some lower-income taxpayers qualify for a lower rate. Starting in 2000 investments that you hold at least five years will be eligble for lower rates (see the "Taxes: A Burden They Have in Common" section of Chapter 6).

When the fund sells shares it has owned less than a year at a profit, you're taxed at the *short-term rate*. That's the same as your ordinary income-tax rate is. If you're in the 28 percent bracket, for example, that's the tax that will be applied to your portion of the profit. Obviously, it's better to be taxed at the long-term rate.

Further, mutual funds generate interest and dividends like individual stocks and bonds. That income is taxed at ordinary rates, which go as high as 39.6 percent for federal taxes.

For many fund shareholders, their lack of control is what annoys them most about such taxes. You and other shareholders can't decide whether a fund will incur such taxes. It's entirely up to the fund manager, who determines when his or her fund will sell shares and generate a tax bill. Worse, you owe tax on capital-gains and income even if the shares of the fund itself (as opposed to the stocks and bonds it owes) fall in value. Talk about the worst of both worlds!

Of course, selling shares in the fund triggers cap-gains taxes at either the long- or short-term rate.

got to do work. Basically, you've got to do all the work that otherwise you'd be leaving in the hands of a fund manager. The bulk of that work consists of wrestling with key decisions. Now *you're* the one who'd have to figure out:

- ✔ Which are the emerging sectors of the Internet economy?
- ✔ Which companies are the dominant market leaders in their fields?
- ✔ Which corporations look to be as popular as prom kings and queens—that is, which have revenues and earnings that are growing at an accelerating clip, which will make them increasingly attractive to investors?
- ✔ Which leading companies' stock price is beaten down by temporary circumstances that are about to be remedied, enabling the stock to soar?
- ✔ Which leading companies look like irresistible bargains? Those are the companies who stock price is temporarily beaten down. Can you spot a remedy for that depressed share price already in the works, which will enable the stock to soar?

That can add up to a lot of work. If you've got a job and a life, you may prefer a more convenient approach to Internet investing. That's where funds enter the picture.

Instead of having to make those calculations listed above:

- ✔ You can delegate stock-picking to a professional investor backed by a team of professional analysts and researchers.
- ✔ You can cut your risks by getting built-in diversification. Investing in a fund, your money is spread among many companies' stocks instead of focused on a vulnerable few.
- ✔ If you're feeling ambitious, you can target a hot sector of the Internet through a specialized fund. You leave it up to the fund

to select the best investments within that sector. Just settle into your seat, and leave the driving up to the fund.

Further, there's no reason you can't mix and match. For instance, what if you've identified one or two stocks that you'd like to invest in, but you don't want to bet the house on them? You could put, say, 25 percent of the money you're willing to devote to the Internet in those individual stocks. You could put the balance of your cash into a broad Internet fund.

Step 6: Fine-Tune Your Strategy

If you decide to invest at least some of your money through funds, then you must decide how broadly to spread your money. Investing in a mutual fund of any kind gives you more diversification than you'd get by investing in only one or a few stocks. But you can diversify more or narrow your investment, depending on which one or more types of funds you select. You've got three choices—broad funds, moderately diversified funds, and narrowly specialized funds:

1. *Specialized* funds typically focus on a single sector of the Internet or on two closely related sectors, such as wireless and telecommunications. Some funds specialize in companies of a specific size—small, medium, large—regardless of their line of business. By investing in only one or two of these funds, you reduce your diversification. That makes you more vulnerable to the ups and downs of whatever types of companies those funds specialize in.
2. The *broad* category includes funds that invest across much or all of the Internet. Investing in broad funds increases your diversification. You can achieve a similar risk reduction by investing in many different types of specialized funds. Combined, they give you diversification. That way, no matter which segments of the Internet are doing well or badly, your money is automatically allocated among all of them.

3. The *middle ground* is occupied by funds that are neither comprehensive nor pinpointed. A fund like this commonly invests in several segments of the Net. It may or may not stick to the same segments all the time. Its official declaration of strategy (found in the prospectus) may be to go anywhere—change its stripes to take advantage of whatever opportunities it spots, wherever it spots them.

Within each of those categories, you'll see funds that perform differently. How can that be? Because they differ from each other not only in terms of specific stocks they choose, but types of stocks they're willing to choose. One fund, for instance, may prefer only large companies. These large craft are steadier in rough seas. But the price for that stability is slower growth. They can't accelerate quickly or grow fast. Another fund may be willing to invest in companies of all sizes.

No matter which category you choose, you must further decide whether you want a fund run by a manager or team of managers who *actively* make investment decisions, or whether you're content to leave your money in an index, flying on autopilot. This sort of fund invests only in stocks on its chosen list or index. The manager is not allowed to make subjective decisions about which stocks look most promising according to whatever criteria the fund uses. You'll recall from Chapter 7 that such funds use a *passive* management.

Yet another way to fine-tune your strategy is by investing in a fund that doesn't specialize in the Internet. By investing in a general technology or telecommunications fund you would be diluting your dependency on the Internet. That would probably reduce your investment's decline during a slump in the Internet sector. But it would deprive you of the greatest possible returns when the Internet outperforms other sectors of the stock market.

The easiest way to tell a general technology fund from an Internet fund is by checking its prospectus or web site. Simply read what the fund says its investment objectives and strategy are. If the fund specializes in the Internet, it will say so. Printed or online reports by fund-analysis services like Morningstar Inc.'s can tell you the same thing.

Both types of funds are free to invest in similar things. It's simply a matter of how they define stocks they buy. Both, for example, can invest in companies that make computers and software. But a Net fund is far more likely to invest in a company that sells, say, dog food or groceries on the Internet. A tech-fund manager might think of such a company as a retailer rather than as a technology firm.

In the description of its investment strategy or approach, if a tech fund doesn't spell out how heavily invested in the Internet it is, check a few things:

- ✔ How do newspapers, magazines, and investment web sites describe it?
- ✔ Does it invest in industries or businesses that are Internet related? For instance, a company that manufactures routers and servers makes equipment that runs the Internet. Even if it isn't labeled as an Internet company, that's what it is. Check Chapter 3 in this book to review the types of businesses that are involved with the Internet.
- ✔ Compare the tech fund's list of stocks with several Internet funds' holdings. Any stocks you see on both lists are obviously Net stocks.
- ✔ Check a company's web site or annual report. The Internet is still hip and novel enough to prompt companies to declare themselves as Net firms if they are.

Step 7: Obey the Dos and Don'ts of Fund Investing

One of the biggest mistakes that fund investors make is to choose a fund based on its past performance. That's understandable.

So many of the available statistics and ratings for funds highlight past performance. And advertisements harp on how well funds have done. Sure, fund companies give lip service to the folly of relying on that by including warnings in their ads, reminding investors that past performance is no guarantee of future success. But those notices always seem to be in microscopic print, don't they? And why are they always tucked away in a bottom corner of the ad?

The truth is different. Studies repeatedly have shown that top-performing diversified stock funds each year have trouble returning to the winner's circle the next year. So rather than betting on a fund that's hot one year, you should invest in funds that have built a solid record of long-term consistency. Go with funds whose average yearly return over three to five years or more is among the top, say, 5 percent or 10 percent, under certain circumstances: Their strategies for success have not changed. The same manager or team is running the fund, the fund's investment approach is the same, and whatever the fund typically invests in is still generating good results.

With Internet funds, that's a little harder. None were around before 1996, so none have had a very long time to demonstrate consistency. But the basic rules of thumb remain the same:

- ✔ Don't invest in yesterday's heroes. Invest in funds with the ability to continue long-running superiority. The easiest way to do that is by putting money into one or more funds that invest broadly in the Internet or in a cross-section of the entire field.
- ✔ Invest in an underlying trend. Rather than invest in a fund that happened to make someone's top-10 funds for the past month or quarter, invest in one or more funds that focus on an area of the Internet that will outperform other sectors. But use this approach only if you're willing to work harder than you'll have to by investing in a broad Internet fund.
- ✔ Don't invest in *yesterday's* hot sector.
- ✔ Invest with winners. That is, put your money into the hands of fund managers (and their researchers) with proven experience and expertise investing in technology.

Some fund managers have had spectacular success investing in the Internet, but not necessarily over the long haul. In Chapter 7 we pointed out fund managers who've done well long-term investing in the technology overall—the Net's parent sector. Here are several of them again. You can review what experience they've had by turning back to that chapter. These aren't the only people you should consider entrusting your money to. But these are the people to measure everyone else against.

RS Internet Age Fund comanagers Jim Callinan and Cathy Baker.

Enterprise Internet Fund manager David Alger.

Firsthand e-Commerce Fund manager Kevin Landis.

Goldman Sachs Internet Tollkeeper lead manager Herbert Ehlers.

Amerindo Technology comanagers Alberto Vilar and Gary Tanaka.

Step 8: Profit from Profits

Generally, stock prices reflect their companies' revenues and earnings. Stocks rise or fall, in line with the company's ability to generate profits for owners, create paychecks for executives and other employees, and attract buyers.

In the most basic terms, a company's value divided by the number of shares gives you its stock price. But that value is almost always based on much more than a single year's worth of profits or even gross revenues. It generally reflects how much larger investors expect *future* revenues and earnings will be.

Periodically, stock prices get inflated by waves of excessive optimism. But sooner or later they retreat to an amount that reflects what people are willing to pay for real businesses.

That sort of reality check is what happened in March 2000. When the technology sector in general—and the Internet in particular—crashed then, investors changed their approach to Internet investing. A period of excessive optimism closed. Investors stopped treating all Internet companies as if they were about to make profits, and large ones at that.

Instead, investors began to focus on companies clearly capable of making money and earning profits. The most popular Internet businesses were suddenly those doing things like building, supplying, or installing hardware and software for the Internet.

After the bubble burst in the spring of 2000, investors were demanding, "Show me the money!"

But the fact that most investors began to focus more on profitability doesn't mean all investors only put money into companies with current profits. One investor still willing to wait for profits was Jacob Internet Fund, as you saw in Chapter 12. It continued to invest in companies based on their future potential.

Like that fund, one of your basic strategy decisions is this: How long are you willing to wait for companies to prove themselves?

You may want to see immediate earnings in stocks you buy, or like Jacob Internet you may be willing to wait. Chances are, the longer you wait the more of a payback you'll want as a reward for letting businesses work with your money. You'll demand a higher return from your investment. After all, time is money. And you'll expect an extra reward for taking a higher risk. Whether your deadline for profitability is short or long, your decision should be based on the underlying investments' ability to create profits.

We'll take a closer look at how to interpret revenues and profits in Chapter 14.

Step 9: Look for Winners in Winning Segments

When asked why he robbed banks, noted felon Willie Sutton famously replied, "Because that's where the money is."

You should apply the same logic. At least when it comes to investing in the Internet. When you're looking for companies with sales and profits, follow the money.

You'll find that in up-and-coming segments of the Internet. That's because companies whose goods and services are growing in popularity faster than others' stand to enjoy accelerating revenues and earnings. Quickening sales and profits lure investors the way chum draws hungry sharks. And that drives up the value of stock.

So Step 8, screening companies for those with accelerating revenues and earnings, is the most direct way to find corporations whose stocks are due to rise. But it's not the only way. You can also bird-dog profits by tracking down ripening market areas. Those are the banks where you'll find money. And that's an approach we'll look at more in Chapter 14.

Step10: Know When to Hold and When to Fold

"Fish and visitors smell in three days," said Benjamin Franklin. His point was that all good things come to an end. It's true for friends whose company grows stale. And it will apply to the Internet too.

The reason the Internet is exciting now is because it is a young field growing rapidly. Companies are spending fortunes to equip themselves for business on the Net. Companies meeting that seemingly insatiable demand are enjoying skyrocketing sales and profits. And those numbers are what drive stock prices up.

There are so many participants: businesses that supply the cables of metal or glass that carry the rising tide of data transmissions; companies that build computers to route and store all of this information traffic; firms whose software can coordinate this flood of messages.

But eventually the initial feeding frenzy will abate. The nonstop construction of everything from transmission towers to cable conduits and back rooms to store computers will slow down. Companies that had no equipment and no software before will finally have their first or second generations of infrastructure in place. Only occasional updates, repairs, and replacements will be needed.

Then this field will shift into a more moderate middle age. Sales and profits will no longer build irresistibly like the storm surge of a hurricane. Fewer companies will be able to vie for the remaining business. And stock prices will not rise like a rocket taking off for earth orbit.

This industry's companies and their stocks will resemble the rest of the economy's. Sales, profits, and stock appreciation will be less dramatic. At that point, you will have to be careful to not be stuck holding stock in losers. And you may find faster-growing investment opportunities elsewhere.

When will the music stop in this game of musical chairs?

"Of course no one can say exactly," says Cathy Baker, comanager of RS Internet Fund. "But it's a good guess that this industry will reach middle age in eight to ten years."

Chapter 14

Basics of Picking Individual Stocks

Remember when you played in your first varsity soccer game? (Or started your first league match for the chess club?) Some senior who'd been at it longer than you may have offered you sage advice: Be scared when the contest starts.

The fact of the matter is, that's *still* a sound warning even once you're an adult and you're about to pit yourself against all the other investors in the world. Think about it: It's you against the world. And this time it's for money, not just bragging rights and a varsity jacket (cool as one may be).

Come to think of it, it *is* for bragging rights as well as money and all the things that can buy, including a wardrobe full of cool threads, not just one varsity jacket.

Being scared means starting with the right frame of mind. Don't take your goal for granted. Don't underestimate your opponents. And don't forget that winning takes effort. Much of that effort goes into the steps required to pick individual stocks successfully.

Let's start with the basics.

NO NEED TO REINVENT THE WHEEL

Investing in stocks requires the same initial steps as investing in mutual funds. You must:

1. Identify your goals.
2. Calculate an overall budget.
3. Figure out how much you can invest.
4. Determine how large your bet on the Internet should be.
5. Decide whether to invest in stocks only, mutual funds, or both.

In Chapters 1 through 13 you learned about the factors that go into those decisions. You must consider things like what your time horizon is. You must also ask yourself such questions as how large your salary is. How much is left over after paying for regular living expenses? Do you need to set aside money to meet any special spending goals? How comfortable are you with investment risks?

If you decide to invest only in mutual funds, you can keep reading this book simply for the sake of intellectual stimulation or to see if you change your mind. But if stocks figure in your investment strategy, then you've got to zero in on the companies whose stock is right for you.

FINDING FUTURE STARS

Choosing individual investments is like being a detective working a murder mystery. You've got to narrow down the list of suspects until you get your man—or, in this case, your stock.

Think of the process as a funnel: It's wide at one end, where you start your pursuit. After all, at the outset your list of potential investments includes all technology stocks as well as stocks in nontechnology companies that could harness the Net to expand business. But your list of prospects becomes increasingly narrow as you get closer to nabbing someone.

The question, of course, is how do you winnow the list, getting rid of stocks you don't want, keeping the ones you do? The answer—as any hard-boiled private eye would tell you—is to follow the money. Generally, companies whose stock prices rise are among those whose revenues and earnings climb. The market smiles on businesses whose sales and profits increase. So to find companies like that in the Internet industry, look for increasingly prosperous corporations.

Fortunately, you don't have to check out each and every tech stock. You can take some shortcuts to find the right ones.

EMERGING SECTORS

You can find a lot of the soon-to-be hottest stocks in the Internet niches that are hottest and heating up. Start your search by identifying the emerging sectors of the Internet.

There are two sets of clues. First, pay attention to the news. You know what the sectors are now. We described them in Chapter 3, and we've discussed them throughout this book. Consider making a file folder for each one. Every day you'll come across news stories online or in print newspapers and magazines, describing the prospects for various sectors. These exercises in crystal-ball gazing will forecast which sectors are heading up, and which are tanking.

Their predictions will be based on larger economic tides, the ebb and flow of demand for various products and services, technological breakthroughs.

Clip and save the Internet trend stories that seem to make the most sense, and file them in the appropriate folder. Periodically, sit back and think about how they tie together. Eventually, you'll see for yourself which trends actually start to emerge.

Scouting Sectors by the Numbers

A second way of homing in on emerging sectors is by the numbers. In a variety of ways publications identify industry groups whose performance is advancing. *Investor's Business Daily (IBD)*, for example, publishes a table ranking industry groups 1 through 197, based on performance of stocks in each one. The ranking is based on each group's performance during the previous six months.

In addition, the *IBD* table makes it easy to tell which industry groups are *improving* in performance the most and which are deteriorating. The table does that, showing you which groups have forward momentum, by listing each group's ranking at the end of the previous week next to its current ranking. It also lists each group's ranking three months earlier. That way, you can see which groups are heating up. If a group currently in, say, the top 10 was in the top 15 a week earlier and only in the top 50 three months earlier, obviously its stock-price performance is on the upswing.

That is an important tool because it's often more helpful to know which groups are *improving* than which are merely hot at the moment—or which were hot in the immediate past. By showing you which groups are on the rise, you'll know where to look first for individual companies on the upswing.

In contrast, a static snapshot that shows only where groups stand now would merely tell you which industry groups have done well recently. For all you would know, their best days may be over. Highly ranked groups may in fact start to head downward. By drawing your attention to highly ranked categories without indicating current direction, a one-dimensional ranking would be showing off yesterday's corporate heroes, not necessarily tomorrow's.

Another way the table is helpful is by highlighting in boldface the 10 groups whose performance on the previous market day alone was best. The 10 worst groups are underlined.

Size Matters

The number of stocks in each group in the *IBD* table described above is also indicated. That's important because the larger a group is, the more significant any movement up or down is. A small group can move up or down on quirky factors. But it takes a lot of money to move a large group of companies. A lot of stock must be bought or sold. If the market is boosting a big sector, that could be a sign that professional investors are optimistic about what's happening in that industry group. If the smart money likes a sector, maybe you should too.

There's a second reason it's good to know whether an industry group is big. It suggests whether the market for each company in the group is big. That's good to know because a big market can help produce big revenues and big profits. Also, a big market gives a company lots of room to expand its sales and profits. And it's easier for a company to increase revenues and profits relatively rapidly if it's doing well despite having only a small percentage of its overall market.

Sectors on the Move

Finally, the *IBD* table tells you how much each group's stock has moved in a specified period of time.

This table is on the last page inside the front section of the newspaper. Nearby on that page is a second, related table, showing companies whose stocks have hit new highs or lows for the past 52 weeks. Not only does this identify individual stocks on the move up or down, it also categorizes them by industry groups. This shows you which industry groups have the most stocks advancing to new high ground or the most retreating.

A third table, generally also on that same page, summarizes which groups have the largest percentage of stocks reaching new highs. It's a third way of telling you which industry sectors are on the uptrend.

Some of these groups may be in Internet businesses or businesses related to it. Some may have nothing to do with the Net. In the table listing all 197 industry groups, you can look up Internet-specific and Internet-related groups by name. Then you can see exactly how well or poorly they're doing.

Factors Fueling Sector Movements

The tables described above can be a key tool in your search for emerging Net sectors.

To find out *why* a sector is advancing or declining, read your daily newspaper's wrapup of each day's stock market activity or catch the day's market wrapup on CNBC or PBS's "Nightly Business Report." By following the forces moving the overall market, you'll have a better feel for what's moving individual sectors and industries, including the Internet. You should check out the paper's tables and graphs that plot the daily ups and downs of the major indices as well. How did the Dow Jones Industrials do yesterday, for example? Did the S&P 500 Index move in the same direction? The paper's daily market summary report will typically comment on that and point out the reasons why.

Likewise, see if your paper publishes a diary of other market sectors' indices. For example, *IBD* publishes a chart of the Nasdaq Composite's daily performance, including lots of vital stats, along with the S&P 500 and Dow Industrials. But it also provides a table showing the performance of indices for sectors of the overall market. That table tracks the daily fortunes of the Nasdaq OTC, high-tech stocks, and the U.S. defense industry to name a few. The paper produces individual charts for several of those indices as well.

Finally, check those file folders we recommended for news stories about Internet industry groups. If you have access to an online archive of news stories, scout through that for relevant news reports.

Sometimes you can get a new perspective on why an individual Internet sector is on the rise or decline by reviewing reports as a group in chronological order. Trends can be clearer over time than when first reported. It's like the difference between a movie and a snapshot. It's easier to understand where a sector is going when you can see the action taking place.

DOMINANT COMPANIES

Once you've identified sectors of the Internet that have the best, most improving stock performance, you know where to start your search for individual winners.

But how do you narrow down your hunt? After all, there are thousands of companies whose stock is publicly traded on the exchanges. You've got more than 400 Internet companies to choose from. They come in all shapes and sizes, in a variety of business segments. Some are famous, but most are obscure. A frightening number are selling on the stock market for only a fraction of the price they fetched on their first day as a publicly traded company.

Don't panic. One way to start is by looking up the companies whose names appear in news stories as leaders in emerging sectors or as examples of good things happening in emerging sectors.

A second place to look is at a table, like the one in *IBD* described above, of stocks reaching new 52-week highs. Remember, the companies are grouped by industry. You don't have to know the names of companies throughout the Internet's many sectors. You can look them up by their sectors. On any given day, you'll find it easy to spot groups such as "Internet," "Electronics," and "Computers."

As you look up the individual companies listed, news stories and online profiles typically mention their counterparts and competitors, which expands your list. Follow through by reading them, so you can see why one company is prospering while another isn't.

Mutual funds provide a third source of indicators of leading companies and sectors whose fortunes are accelerating. Identify funds that specialize in Net sectors that are advancing. Then look at their holdings. Which ones are doing best?

Remember, funds periodically reveal their holdings and even describe the ones helping and hurting them the most. Look for those reports. Check a fund or fund family's web site, where they may provide updated information. You can even look up each stock in a fund's portfolio in the newspaper or online. See how it's doing. Investigate news stories and online forums where fund managers are interviewed and describe their latest tactics. These are often excellent sources of information that's more up-to-date than the fund's own official portfolio list.

In addition, look for features like the graphs of leading mutual funds in *IBD's* mutual funds section. Internet funds and broader technology funds appear here along with other types of mutual funds. The graphs show the most recently reported stocks being bought and sold by these funds. The graphs also show each fund's favorite stocks. If you're looking for help in identifying promising individual stocks, what better way than by seeing what Wall Street professionals are putting their money into?

A related feature in the Friday mutual fund section shows which industry groups and individual stocks are being accumulated by an entire fund family. Spotlighting a different fund family each week, the group's stock buys are listed by name and by industry sector.

A chart shows how the group's investment in each top holding has changed over the most recent reporting periods—is the fund family buying or selling? And an accompanying story describes and analyzes those bets. The story typically provides commentary by a fund manager or investment strategist at the group.

LOOK FOR GROWTH

When you've identified key companies and leading Internet sectors, it's time to figure out which of those companies would make the best investments. Do that by putting together things you've learned during your search. Look for three things:

1. Leading companies *in* fast-growing sectors of the Internet.
2. Companies with outstanding growth of both earnings and revenues.
3. Companies that have institutional support.

Market Leaders

Look at market leadership first. One reason it's important is because big companies have better resources for defending themselves and for expanding their sales and profits. They can afford to do more of the things that typically help corporations: research, marketing, improving techniques to cut costs, taking over competitors and allies that can be helpful, slashing their own prices to defend market share.

Market leadership is also important because customers like to buy from brand-name producers. Customers trust brand names. They expect better service and support from brand names. That gives these companies sales momentum. As a result, the bulk of sales and profits in any line of business tends to go to that sector's market leaders.

It's important to see not only whether a company is a leader, but also whether it is poised to remain dominant. That's where rising earnings and sales come into the picture. They are your clearest, most direct barometer of where a company is going.

Companies on the Fast Track

Don't focus on big companies alone, though. Your main target is companies that are fast-growing. A company that is merely dominant may in fact be past its prime. It may be growing slowly if at all. It may no longer be capable of doing things in business that attracted investors in the first place. Its stock may be as high as it will go—or at least at a level where it no longer will rise fast.

So your primary focus should be on fast-growing companies. Market leadership is merely a way of identify which ones those are. Stock in a small, fast-growing company may rise much faster than a big firm that's seen better days.

When it comes to sales and profits, watch for firms whose revenues and profits are growing at a 25 percent pace. That sounds simple enough, and it is. But you should keep certain fine points in mind:

- ✔ *Profits* are earnings—in this case earnings per share. Earnings per share are a company's total after-tax profits divided by the company's number of shares outstanding, which means the shares held by all shareholders (generally excluding stock repurchased by the company).

  Shares outstanding is a common vital statistic, which is easy to find. Don't confuse it with the *float*, which refers to the number of shares outstanding minus those owned by management or other people such as company founders. The float is the number of shares usually available for buying and selling by you and other investors who are members of the general public.

✔ What you should watch for is the increase in earnings in the current business quarter compared with the same quarter a year earlier. Far less important—in fact, potentially confusing and misleading—is any change in the current quarter versus the quarter immediately before it.

The reason you should compare the same quarters in subsequent years is that that shows you how the company did during the same season. It filters out seasonal fluctuations from your comparison. It shows how the company did under similar conditions, during the same time in its yearly business cycle, with a year's more experience (and, the company hopes, with larger accumulated resources to put to use).

Many companies, for example, rack up lots of extra sales during the traditional holiday season, which is during the fourth quarter. For such companies, if you compare fourth-quarter earnings to those in the third quarter you should see a big jump in sales and profits. But what if the company actually did better the previous year? By comparing consecutive quarters rather than quarter-versus-year ago, you'd miss seeing that alarming trend.

✔ Also, look for accelerating earnings. That means checking to see whether the rate of earnings growth in recent quarters (compared with the corresponding quarters a year earlier) increased. In other words, was the pace of earnings growth larger each recent quarter?

For example, suppose the most recent quarter was the second quarter, and hypothetical company XYZ Corp.'s earnings increased by 35 percent versus the second quarter in the prior year. If the first-quarter rate was 30 percent and the previous quarter, the fourth in the year before, was 25 percent, and the third quarter was 20 percent, that forms a pattern of accelerating earnings growth. That's good.

- ✔ Don't be fooled by increases that are large but only because they are in comparison with puny earnings or even losses in the same quarter a year earlier.

  For example, if a company's quarterly earnings are 11 cents versus one cent a year earlier, that's a 1,000 percent increase. Sounds impressive. But a penny-a-share profit is barely any profit at all. A company whose quarterly earnings jump to $2 from $1 a year earlier may have an increase of *only* 100 percent, but it's obviously in better shape than the company earning 11 cents.

  In contrast, the company earning 11 cents is dangerously close to slipping back into red ink. On the other hand, if its earnings in subsequent quarters go to, say, 30 cents, then 70 cents, followed by $1, you may be looking at a real comer.

- ✔ Don't just scratch the surface. Look at how a company has done for several quarters.

- ✔ Don't settle for comparisons of the current six- or nine-month period versus the same period a year ago. Decent numbers for an extended period could make a company's outlook appear rosy while in truth masking a deteriorating performance in the most recent three-month period.

- ✔ Check for nonrecurring profits. Those are profits from onetime events, which the company can't count on repeating. Because they don't result from ongoing, regular business operations, they may puff up a company's numbers in one quarter, but then they're likely to disappear.

  Suppose ABC Corp., a hypothetical company that makes routers, sells some land and buildings where it used to make machines that aren't as good as its competition's. You should subtract the profit from that sale from its quarterly earnings report. If you can't do it yourself, watch how news accounts, financial web sites, and the company's own reports explain the adjustment.

- ✔ Look for at least roughly similar rates of increase in both quarterly sales and earnings. If sales are increasing much faster than earnings, find out why. It's one thing if a company is plowing sales back into itself, paving the way for greater future profits. But it's not so good if a company is wrestling with an ongoing drain on earnings. For example, does it have an old plant that requires an expensive environmental cleanup and closure of a factory? Read quarterly reports, annual reports, and news accounts to get a feel for a company's circumstances.

Likewise, what if sales growth is flat but profits are well up anyway? Sounds good, right? After all, management must be making the most out of revenues. But what if a company is boosting profits by, say, laying off workers? That doesn't bode well for the future.

- ✔ Look for increases in annual earnings too. That confirms any good news you see in quarterly reports.

  But if a company that has been in business many years shows a sudden falloff in annual earnings in any recent year, find out why. This is a double-check on quarterly earnings growth. It's also a way of looking further back into a company's stability than recent quarters alone will show.
- ✔ Look beneath the surface. Many investors wrongly assume that very young companies don't have earnings data predating their respective initial public offerings. That's not true. You can find earnings figures for companies from when they were privately held in company prospectuses.
- ✔ Understand a company's business. That may sound so obvious that it doesn't need to be said. But as you examine candidate stocks, make a point of clarifying in your own mind what each company does. Understanding what products and services a company offers can help put into sharper focus the competitive forces that shape its financial results. This should help you understand each company's sales and profit performance.

Helpful Indicators

Once you find companies that meet those requirements, check for factors that will continue to buoy their stock prices:

- ✔ *High earnings per share rating.* On your own, you can look at whether a company's earnings are growing. It also helps to know how a company's earnings growth compares with other companies'. *IBD* provides a tool for doing precisely that in its stock tables. The *Earnings Per Share (EPS) Rating* measures each company's earnings growth over several time periods, and shows you how that merged calculation stacks up against other companies'.

  The EPS Rating is based largely on the percent change in the past two quarters' earnings in comparison with the same quarters a year earlier. A company's three- to five-year annual growth rate is also factored in, but without as much weight. The equation's combined result gives an overall relative earnings rating.

  That figure is compared with all the other companies in the newspaper's stock tables ranked on a scale of 1 to 99. A 99 EPS Rating means a company's earnings growth beats 99 percent of all other companies tracked.

- ✔ *Strong relative price strength.* You can look up a stock's price. You can also see how it compares with its own 52-week high and low. In addition, *IBD*'s stock tables provide a measurement that shows how that stock price's movement compares to other stocks'.

  Like the EPS rating, this proprietary measurement ranks stock behavior on a scale from 1 to 99. A *Relative Strength* of 99 means the stock's price change (presumably a gain) has been better than 99 percent of all other stocks over the past 12 months. Market leaders generally rank at least 80 in both EPS and Relative Strength Ratings.

- ✔ *Return on equity (ROE).* This is another barometer of financial performance. It shows how efficiently a company uses its investors' money. As *IBD* founder Bill O'Neil puts it, this measures a company's bang per buck. Basically, it is calculated by dividing annual net income by stockholders' equity.

  Improvements in productivity, which cuts costs, typically push ROE higher. Look for an ROE of 17 percent or higher. A company with an ROE of 20 percent or higher is probably a leader in its field, O'Neil says. Only the fastest growing companies, which includes some young Internet firms, have ROEs as high as 40 percent to 50 percent.

High ROE, Relative Strength, and EPS Rating don't by themselves push up stock prices. But they are indicators of strong business performance and financial health, which are characteristics investors seek. Healthy numbers in these measurements are often predecessors of rising stock prices.

✔ *New development.* Startling gains in stock price are often sparked by a new development. It could be a company's introduction of a new product or service, or new top management. For instance, Wang Labs stock began a huge run up in 1978 thanks to the creation of its new word-processing office machines, O'Neil notes in one of his books on investing.

You can find news about developments in your daily paper. You should also scout through the web site of any company you've identified as a leader with earnings and sales growth. Financial web sites and trade publications are other sources for leads on new products, services, and management moves.

✔ *Institutional support.* That's a fancy term that refers to whether mutual funds, banks, insurance companies, and other large investors are putting money into a stock. Institutional support is important because these heavy hitters control about 80 percent of the money in the market, according to *IBD*. Take away 80 percent of its air, and most creatures choke. With enough air, a stock can breathe and flourish.

One place where you can see whether a stock is favored by these deep-pocketed investors is in *IBD*'s stock tables. On Tuesdays, the tables include a column showing what it calls *Sponsorship Rating*. The size and quality of institutional support for each stock is rated on a scale of A to E. An A or B rating indicates two things: Better-performing mutual funds own a lot of the stock; and, the number of funds investing in the stock has risen in recent quarters.

✔ *Rising volume.* What happens when a tubby kid jumps into a swimming pool? He makes a big splash. The same thing happens when lots of investors, especially big ones like mutual funds, jump into a stock. They make a visible impact.

The importance of heavy volume is that it indicates interest by institutional investors. Their combined purchasing power can lift the price of a stock. It can also signal the start of a sustained ascent by a stock. If you buy what the big boys buy, your stock is likely to climb.

Likewise, pack selling can depress a stock's price. You must decide whether to sell some or all of your shares, or hunker down for the long haul if your research convinces you that the stock can rebound within a time period acceptable to you. Also, stocks whose prices rally but only on modest volume often have trouble continuing their climb.

You can spot institutional buying when a stock's price rises on heavy trading volume. (Ditto for institutional selling: Share price falls on heavy volume.) Many major newspapers' business sections provide lists of stocks that were the previous day's or week's most actively traded.

For example, in its Stock Market Data Bank inside the "Money & Investing" section, the *Wall Street Journal* lists the stocks whose shares were the most traded on the prior market day, those that made the biggest percentage gains, and those with the largest price jumps or declines. The paper's stock tables list each issue's volume. Stocks whose volume was among their respective exchange's heaviest are underlined.

IBD's tables include each stock's percentage volume change, above or below its 50-trading-day average, as well as the volume itself. When volume climbs 50 percent or more, it is printed in boldface. One column in the tables shows *IBD*'s *Accumulation/Distribution Rating*. This feature ranks each stock, based on its daily price and volume changes for the past 13 weeks. An A or B rating indicates moderate-to-heavy buying. C shows that buying and selling have been about equal. D and E indicate that selling has been moderately to heavily greater than buying.

In addition, the paper's "Where The Big Money's Flowing" feature at the start of the New York Stock Exchange main tables lists stocks with the previous day's largest percentage increase in trading volume. This saves you the effort of scanning the stock tables themselves, picking out stocks one by one. And since readers of this book want to focus on Internet stocks, you can look for Net stocks alone in this feature.

Only stocks whose price change was at least 50 cents on heavy volume are listed. The table is also limited to those stocks whose shares cost at least $18, so it reflects only stocks that institutional buyers can afford. Penny stocks need not apply. This way, you're examining stocks that stand the best chance of being lifted by a rising water level when fat kids enter Wall Street's swimming pool.

Other data, like each stock's price change, its price/earnings ratio, and how well its industry group is faring, are also listed in the "Big Money" feature.

A nearby daily feature, "The Real Most Active," analyzes individual heavy-volume traders in more depth. You'll often find Internet stocks here. This feature explains why a particular stock is enjoying rising volume.

Why so many tools for spotting and then dissecting stocks with rising volume? Because, in addition to the reasons explained above, winning stocks commonly enjoy escalating volume even before their share prices start big climbs. Heavy volume can also signal mass exodus from a troubled stock. But rising volume should be one of several indicators you use to zero in on leading stocks.

PRICING A COMPANY'S STOCK

What price is too high? That question is on every investor's mind. As Internet stocks became more popular, a furious debate emerged over whether some share prices were in fact too high. Investors who felt certain stocks were overvalued sold them or refused to buy them in the first place. They felt vindicated when the technology and Internet sectors sagged in the spring of 2000. But in the meantime they had missed out on those sectors' enormous gains.

So how much is too much when it comes to paying share price?

One of the most popular measurements is the *price/earnings (p/e) ratio*. As its name indicates, it is calculated by dividing a stock's price by its annual per-share earnings. The ratio shows how much higher a stock's price is than its earnings per share. It translates stock price into a multiple of earnings.

In other words, if a company's earnings this year total $1.50 and its share price is $12, its p/e ratio is 8. Investment professionals will say that this company is trading at 8 times earnings, or that its stock price trades at a multiple of 8 times the company's annual earnings (or, in shorthand jargon, at a multiple of 8).

But a p/e ratio is more than just accountants' gobbledygook. It shows how much you have to pay for a given company's earnings. The higher the ratio, the higher the cost of that company's earnings. You want to buy shares in a profitable company? It costs. The more earnings it has, the higher the cost.

The calculation, by the way, uses net earnings, which are profits remaining after things like taxes, operating expenses, interest on bonds (rare for young Internet companies), and dividends (also rare) have been paid.

Obviously, the ratio fluctuates whenever a stock's price moves or its earnings change. It's easy to calculate a stock's p/e ratio. But you'll rarely have to. It's widely included in newspaper stock tables and in stock research reports.

You can put any stock's p/e ratio into perspective quickly and easily. Simply compare it with its competitors' p/e ratios, with its industry group's p/e ratio, and with the market overall. If the stock's p/e ratio is higher, what makes you think it deserves that?

For example, right now the p/e ratio of the S&P 500 Index is about 37. If you're considering a stock with a p/e ratio of, say, 45, what makes you think that higher price is justified?

Well, aside from looking at its competitors and its industrial sector, you could answer that question simply by looking at its earnings. If they are growing, the stock could *grow into its multiple*, as Wall Streeters would say. In fact, investment pros often calculate p/e ratio in terms of estimated future or *forward* earnings (that is, generally, earnings for the next 12 months or the current fiscal year), rather than merely relying on historical or past earnings.

But a simpler justification is in the stock price itself. If supply and demand drive the price up, it's worth it to own the stock. It doesn't take an Internet stock on steroids to do that. As the Motley Fool, a popular financial web site, pointed out in a discussion of stock pricing, Coca-Cola was priced at 46 times earnings in 1972. Even at 95 times earnings it would have topped the return of the S&P 500 over the ensuing 25 years.

The problem with relying solely on pricing yardsticks is that a measurement like p/e ratio—when based on trailing rather than future earnings—describes what a price has done, not what it will do or is expected to do. And with stocks, you get what you pay for. A stock with a low p/e ratio isn't merely cheap; it's a stock that the market doesn't value enough to drive up.

And your goal isn't to save money when you buy stocks. It's to buy stocks that will rise, no matter *what* you pay for them.

Stocks with higher prices get that way because institutional buyers favor them. In fact, institutional buyers often avoid low-priced stocks. That's because they're looking for champions—aren't you too?—and champions are often already commanding higher prices.

That's what *IBD* found when it scanned its database of stocks, examining those with earnings per share and relative price strength of at least 80. As we described above, EPS and RPS are two of the proprietary analysis tools used by the paper. And a rating of 80 means that a stock has beaten 80 percent of all other stocks in those measurements. The paper also screened its database for stocks with at least 1 percent of their stock float owned by mutual funds.

Out of 10,000 stocks, the paper found only 70 priced $5 or less that met those criteria. In other words, mutual funds ignored low-priced stocks even though they had outstanding earnings and solid price climbs. Individual investors were on their own with those.

But the pool of stocks widened to 228 among stocks whose share price was $10 or less. It grew to 415 for stocks $15 or less and 610 for stocks costing $20 or less. There were 1,056 stocks priced $40 or less.

The moral? You can invest your money and wait for your neighbors to drive the price up. Or you can invest in stocks more likely to attract big-spending institutional investors. It's your choice.

Why do institutional investors do that? Because low-priced stocks can be young and untested. They can be from small companies that haven't issued a lot of stock. Those are not inviting qualities to Wall Street. Institutional investors don't want to get stuck with a stock that's not familiar to the rest of Wall Street. That's the sort of stock they can't sell when they want to. They don't want a stock that is cheap because it is stagnating. And they don't want a stock with a tiny float because they can end up driving up the stock's price as they buy it—in effect, driving up their own costs.

It's far better to invest in the best, most popular Net stocks. Your goal isn't to demonstrate how cool you are by finding something different, something *funky*. You want to own something that other investors will buy back from you at a profit precisely because they know what it is and value it—even more than you did.

TECHNICAL ANALYSIS

Stocks often move in predictable patterns. Those patterns can be plotted or charted. You can use a chart as a sort of map to guide your purchase of shares. You wait until the stock has moved through the pattern, positioning itself for its next leg, an upward climb in share price. You shouldn't buy too soon, and you shouldn't buy at all if the stock fails to complete any intermediate steps.

Generally, it is stocks with the characteristics you want that complete the intermediate steps. Those are stocks with earnings growth, sales growth, rising volume, and institutional support.

Here's what happens. No matter how good, stocks typically run out of gas at some point. Whether their share price has been rising briefly or for a long time, sooner or later investors decide to turn their attention elsewhere. Maybe the company's earnings growth has lagged. Maybe sales have flattened. Maybe key executives depart. Maybe the competition makes a striking breakthrough. Whatever the reason, it always happens. No stock goes up without interruption.

That's no surprise to anyone. So should you wait until the stock relapses before buying? How far down do you wait for its share price to slide? Is that little voice inside you saying, *Aha!* Buy low, sell high!

The right point to buy is not while a stock is falling. That surprises some investors, who think of a stock whose price is falling as a bargain. It may be. But the danger is that you may not know for sure *why* it's falling. And you certainly can't know for sure before the fact how *far* it will eventually fall. Your buy-low strategy may turn out to be buying high after all.

The right time is not around the stock's low point, either, say right after it starts to climb again. That's because it may not be attractive enough to keep rising. Earnings and sales may not be growing enough to lure serious investors. Besides, as you learned earlier in this chapter, cheaper is not necessarily better when it comes to putting your money on the line in the market. You want a stock that is healthy enough to draw professional investors. And they're interested in winners, not wounded refugees from the bargain bin.

Quality stocks on the mend commonly fight their way back up to their previous high price. Chartists call this sort of down-and-up path a *cup* pattern. *Surely*, you may think, *that's* the right time to buy. But it's still not. What often happens around the old high is that investors who got caught by surprise on the way down start to sell their shares. They've sweated out the initial decline and recovery, and now they're eager to strap on a parachute and jump. They're happy to escape without losing cash, only time and opportunity. On paper, they've broken even.

Some stocks continue to climb from that point. If you can catch it before it's climbed 5 percent above its old high, go for it. But many stocks start to drift sideways at this point. There are still just enough investors looking to bail out at this break-even level to keep the stock from climbing. The price may even sag slightly This sideways or gently declining movement is referred to as a *handle*. Visually, the overall formation is a *cup-with-a-handle* pattern.

That's not the only pattern. For instance, some stocks fall, rise, and fall again before climbing once more. That's called a *double bottom*. Whatever the specific type of pattern, the entire period from the stock's decline through its complete recovery is its *consolidation*. The best candidates for your shopping basket are those stocks whose consolidation, or base, lasts seven weeks or more.

What happens next to a quality stock is this: Eventually, enough sellers have departed so they're outnumbered by buyers. The price starts to firm. If buyers are sufficiently enthusiastic, volume heats up. On a day of big volume the stock breaks out, darting above its former high price.

This is the time to buy.

Remember, quality means sound fundamentals: earnings growth, sales growth, institutional support, and so on. On a breakout, look for volume to surge as much as 40 percent to 50 percent—more for smaller-cap stocks.

But don't wait long. The optimal point to buy is when share price reaches one-eighth of a percentage point above the top of the handle, says investment veteran Bill O'Neil, who has championed most of the growth-oriented tools discussed in this chapter. That precise point is called its *pivot*. If you miss the pivot point, forget about buying once the share price has risen 5 percent past that. You've missed the safest part of the rebound, O'Neil says. Beyond that, you could be buying shares when the stock is in danger of relapsing.

SELL RULE

Investors wonder whether they should sell stock when either of two things happens: The share price has advanced so much that they've made a bundle on paper, or the share price has fallen enough for them to be afraid of losing a bundle.

Let's look at the scary prospect first. The rule to follow is simple because it relies on easy arithmetic. Once a stock has fallen 7 percent to 8 percent below whatever you paid, get out. That's not because the stock is necessarily likely to fall further. Instead, it's an uncomplicated defensive tactic, which O'Neil advocates.

Look at the numbers. Suppose you buy a stock at $100 a share, but then it falls to $50. For you to break even, that $50 stock has to add on $50 in value. That would be a 100 percent gain. How many stocks do that quickly? Too few.

But if your $100-a-share stock falls to $93, you'd only need a 7.5 percent rebound to be back to square one. If the initial decline is to $92, an 8.7 percent comeback would get you back to your starting point. Obviously, those smaller recoveries would be easier, more likely, and faster.

If your stock racks up huge gains and then suffers minor setbacks before advancing again, that's different. The 7 percent-to-8 percent sell rule applies only to your original purchase price, not to subsequent high points.

But what if your stock starts to retreat after making big gains? You certainly don't need to wait until you've lost your entire gain and then some before selling. When a full-blown selloff seems to be underway, look at whether the market overall is in a funk. And check the status of your stock's industry group. Watch for individual news stories or consult the industry group vital stats in your newspaper. If the entire sector is pulling back, don't try to buck the trend. Even if your stock's fundamentals are sound—if earnings and revenues are still growing, and so on—it is likely to be pulled down as large investors turn sour on its overall group and sell out indiscriminantly. Instead, take your profit and run.

That way, you'll convert a paper profit to a cash one—the best sort, of course. You can always buy the stock back later as conditions improve. Or you can put that money back to work in another, more promising stock.

This sell rule gives you the best of both worlds: sitting on a profit, and with cash that you can invest in the next quality Internet stock. You may find that next investment the same day, or you may have to wait for the market to firm up. Sooner or later, it always does. Despite the Great Depression, two world wars, the Cold War, the oil embargo of the 1970s, the Red Sox selling Babe Ruth to the Yankees, hoop deity Michael Jordan's retirement, and the proliferation of karaoke, the market has never failed to recover from any affliction, or to survive any setback.

The market knows how to do its part. And now you're one chapter away from being better prepared to take advantage of opportunity.

Chapter 15

How to Use the Web for Research

The Internet is a feast, beckoning investors who are hungry to learn. Better yet, it is a gourmet feast at fast-food prices, served with fast-food speed. It has made available all kinds of investment information, from the carefully prepared proprietary research once reserved for white-shoe clients of Wall Street's elite brokerages to the staples of investment decision making—basic documents like annual reports, which only a few years ago you could acquire only by calling your broker and waiting days for its delivery.

Best of all, it makes all of this available at the click of a mouse button. It is served up whenever you like, day or night, midweek or weekend. Want to nibble at your desk while tending to business tasks? Why not? Prefer home delivery? No problem.

And the Internet makes this dazzling menu of market intelligence available either for free or, at most, for prices that are much lower than they've ever been. That's largely due to the take-no-prisoners struggle between full-service and discount brokerages. To staunch the hemorrhage of their investors to the low-cost competition, full-service brokerages are introducing their own online trading sites and slashing prices for their offline services. Meanwhile, discount brokerages are fighting for market share—for business from investors like you—by offering more and more bells and whistles, at the lowest prices they can bear to levy.

The Internet even offers you the equivalent of your friendly neighborhood bar: chat rooms at financial web sites. There, you can chew the fat with friends and strangers who share your interest in whichever Net firm or trend gets your juices flowing.

Of course, even the best saloons can get rowdy at times, and you've got to protect your wallet. It's like the referee tells boxers before the opening bell; "Keep your guard up at all times." Think about the source of any information you find before relying on it. While you're trying to learn what you can to earn an honest buck, others may be prowling for victims to exploit.

KEEP YOUR DUKES UP

Look how investors got burned by a phony news report that started on the Internet and spread through the investment community with the speed of a million eyeballs perusing online bulletin boards and chatroom conversations.

A 23-year-old community college student, according to authorities, issued a fake press release in August 2000, which said the chief executive of Emulex Corp., a Costa Mesa, California-based maker of fiber-optic equipment, had quit and the company was restating its quarterly earnings from a profit to a loss. The allegedly bogus story was quickly picked up and used by major news outlets. Within minutes the company's stock plunged about 60 percent, even though the news proved to be utterly false. Numerous investors got scorched.

Authorities charged that the student mastermind had lost nearly

$100,000 investing in Emulex. The news release was supposedly meant to drive down the price of Emulex stock. That would enrich the 23-year-old man, who had *shorted* the stock, betting it would drop, authorities said. Then he made more money, reportedly by scarfing up shares once they had plunged in price and riding their rebound after Emulex officials disproved the fake news item.

The case is a reminder that not all information on the Internet is reliable. Not all alleged news even comes from objective sources. Some comes from people who are trying to profit, whether it's by driving up the price of shares they own or by scuttling the share price of stock they've placed bets against.

The lesson is that you should think about the source of any information you find before basing an investment on it. There are more and more info outlets online every week, ranging from financial chat rooms where investors like you gather to swap thoughts, to web sites run by reputable news organizations that have established records for reliability over the course of years.

Stick with the brand names. Or at least take everything, no matter what the source, with the proverbial grain of salt. Before putting your money at risk, ask yourself what you know about the source of information. Do you know for a fact that the source has no conflict of interest? Do you know for a fact that the source is not some irresponsible college sophomore goofing on people? Do you know for a fact that the source is not some disgruntled ex-employee of the firm being discussed, seeking revenge through mayhem? And do you know for a fact that the source isn't some otherwise harmless guy who simply doesn't know what he's talking about?

If you can't answer yes to those questions, don't expose yourself financially.

That still leaves plenty of potentially useful, inexpensive sources of information about Internet and other types of stocks. In previous chapters we've discussed how to use materials like corporate reports and mutual fund prospectuses and semiannual reports. Below are some we haven't discussed. Costs vary widely.

A TREASURE TROVE OF RESEARCH TOOLS

Research

Bloomberg
www.bloomberg.com
This site has a variety of financial and market news, financial analysis, stock quotes, and market results. In addition, it has a section devoted to technology stocks, which includes a feature showing the status of the Bloomberg Internet Index. Prices and changes for a select list of Internet stocks are shown. Also, the index is charted, with its performance during the past month, three months, and year-to-date shown. Another feature shows the status of Internet sectors. The value of each sector and its daily percentage change are listed.

DailyStocks.com
www.dailystocks.com
This site lays claim to being the Web's first and biggest stock research site. Select a stock, for instance, and you can choose from a large list of links to other sites that offer information. Topics range from daily quotes and performance charts to historical quotes, relative strength data, float volume, five-year earnings growth, institutional ownership, and information about the stock's industry group. Plus, this source sports links to a long list of well-known sites providing market commentary. Also, these are links to computerized stock-screening sites.

One section is devoted to technology stocks. It offers links to about 35 electronic publications. A dozen or so focus on the Internet. In turn, one link lists about 30 Internet news, analysis, and commentary sites around the Web, identifying many by the Internet subsectors they focus on.

Edgar
www.sec.gov/edgarhp
This is the Securities and Exchange Commission's Electronic Data Gathering and Retrieval site. Here you can find filings that companies

are required to submit to this agency, which is the U.S. government's watchdog over the investment industry. You can find everything from mutual fund prospectuses to corporate quarterly earnings reports.

FinancialWeb.com

www.financialweb.com

Links to a variety of stock and mutual fund data and commentary. Using the research feature, you can type in the name or ticker symbol of a stock, and the site will show you various brokerage recommendations (with dates) as well as fundamental financial data. A table also appears, listing online news sources that have commented on the stock, summarizing what each said and offering a link to the commentary.

The stocks page shows the market status of various indexes and sectors. When you click on the technology sector, you are linked to a page showing the status of subsectors. Those include numerous Internet-oriented sectors such as Internet software and services as well as networking and communication devices. Click on any of *those*, and you are connected to a table showing the status and performance of stocks making up that group. You can also click on such features as *movers*, and—*presto*—those stocks are organized in order of the ones making the biggest market gains, accompanied by basic info. You can learn more about individual companies by clicking on any one.

FreeEdgar

www.freeedgar.com

Run by a nongovernment firm, this site offers free access to reports filed with the SEC. Generally, this site is easier to navigate and use than the SEC's own site. Also, it offers features that the SEC's Edgar does not, such as arranging for an e-mail heads-up when a company on your watch list files a report with the SEC.

FreeRealTime

www.freerealtime.com

Real-time quotes used to be available only to brokers and other market professionals. Now they're common on the Web, but many charge fees, which range from nominal to hefty. The main attraction of this site is seeing stock quotes in real time (without the delay of 15 or 20 minutes that's common elsewhere) for free. The site also offers such features as news, commentary, and bulletin boards.

Hoover's Online

www.hoovers.com

This site offers profiles of companies and industries. Check the status of your favorite industrial sector, the Internet, and various subsectors. Choose among links to individual companies.

If you're interested in new talent, check out the page that's a jumping-off point for features dealing with initial public offerings.

Investorama

www.investorama.com

You name it, this site has links to it. Investorama offers links to more than 14,000 financial web sites in 240 categories.

Just one of their features: directory and ratings of more than 100 online brokerages.

Investor's Business Daily

www.investors.com

A full-service site, which offers news stories from the printed newspaper as well as such features as stock quotes and a financial glossary. You can also access analytical tools such as the "*IBD* Stock Checkup," which gives you a diagnosis of a stock's fundamentals and how healthy its industry group is. Also available are the "Daily Graphs Online" charts, which present about 70 fundamental and technical indicators for each company.

Investorwords

www.investorwords.com

Want to know the difference between earnings and operating income? This site provides more than 5,000 definitions for general financial terms.

JustQuotes
www.justquotes.com
A cornucopia of links to a wide variety of financial and investment information sites, including sites dealing with earnings, IPOs, daily market results, price gainers, price losers, taxes, mutual funds, and economic data. One section of JustQuotes specializes in technology stocks, and includes links to several sites devoted to Internet stocks.

MSN MoneyCentral
www.moneycentral.msn.com
Produced by software giant Microsoft, this site features a variety of personal finance information. Its investor section has tools for researching individual stocks and mutual funds. Offers links to stock-screening features at Morningstar and Charles Schwab.

Wall Street Journal
www.wsj.com
Site includes news stories and features from the *Journal*. The site also provides links to other web pages, such as one providing corporate earnings estimates and consensus stock price recommendations from First Call/Thomson Financial.

Yahoo!
http://finance.yahoo.com
A very popular site, offering everything from quotes to news, discussion boards, chat rooms, and links to sites that have commentary. You can look up quotes for a specific company, and get news relating to that company.

Zacks Investment Research
www.zacks.com
News and analysis from a variety of sources. The daily market overview lists the performance of various indexes, including several technology-oriented ones as well as the Dow Jones Internet Commerce and Internet Service indices. The site includes a stock-

screening feature, which lets you search for stocks that meet criteria you specify.

Stock and Fund Screens

MarketPlayer

www.marketplayer.com

The site offers stock screening, using up to 100 or more criteria. You can build your own screens, custom-tailoring each to your goals. Or you can use any of the site's ready-made screens. Those prefab screens focus on specific criteria, like companies with low price/earnings ratios. Others focus on investment strategies like value-oriented stock-picking, where you search for companies with little debt and low price-to-book price tags.

The site offers other goodies as well. You can find 12-month forward earnings estimates, bulletin boards, research, and a glossary of financial terms.

MaxFunds

www.maxfunds.com

The site offers screening of funds, with emphasis on small and new funds—which is what many Internet funds are. One feature unique to the site is its projection of how large a fund can grow before its size will start to hurt it. For example, if a fund that specializes in small companies in a tiny industry buys a lot of shares in one company, it can drive up the share price. A fund with such a specialty would start to hurt its own interests once it grows beyond a relatively small asset size.

You'll also find graphics-rich data and down-to-earth analysis.

Morningstar

www.morningstar.com

This popular fund-research organization provides a large number of screening tools, along with its well-known star-studded fund reports.

Quicken.com
www.quicken.com
In this site's investing section, you can screen for stocks or mutual funds either using preset criteria or specifying your own criteria. For example, you can ask the system to show you companies in a specific industry, such as wireless telecommunications, that meet certain size requirements and have whatever growth rate for sales and earnings you indicate. The parent site provides market news and commentary.

Earnings

EarningsWhispers.com
www.earningswhispers.com
This site derives its name from the fact that earnings predictions are known as *whisper numbers*. The site provides news about and announcements from individual companies. Also, you can bring up tables showing each company's quarterly and annual earnings and sales, earnings per share, profit margin, and growth rates along with various data based on earnings. Tables show earnings estimates from Wall Street analysts and the whisper earnings.

Thomson Investor Network
www.thomsoninvest.com
News and analysts' reports on companies and industries. The site offers access to earnings estimates from First Call, which investment professionals use.

Stock Charts

Big Charts
www.bigcharts.com
A service of CBS's Marketwatch.com, this site features static and basic interactive charts. Using drop-down menus, you can customize charts in various ways—by looking at performance over various time periods,

for instance. You can also compare a stock with various indexes and industry groups, including the Internet.

With a click of your mouse button, you can pull up various lists of *movers*—New York Stock Exchange stocks with the biggest percentage gain in price, for example, or Nasdaq stocks hitting new 52-week-high prices.

News about companies is categorized by subject matter, broad themes, and by industry sectors, including the Internet. Individual stock quotes are available. The page offering brokerage reports has a section devoted to Internet stocks.

Daily Graphs Online

www.dailygraphs.com

This tracks 11,000 NYSE, Amex, and Nasdaq companies in the database of William O'Neil & Co., a sister company of *Investor's Business Daily*. The graphs and charts are accompanied by a wealth of detailed but easy-to-understand technical and fundamental data. You can see such information as quarterly earnings and sales growth figures for whichever company you specify. Features also include data related to indices and market indicators. You can also screen for stocks by various criteria.

Prophet Financial Systems

www.prophetfinance.com

Prophet seeks to give users a vision of the financial future. Charts are its main tool in that endeavor, but the site also provides news, market data, and bulletin boards.

Need help finding a particular company? Or finding companies within a sector? In the chart surfer section, you can click on technology to see four constituent subsectors, one of which is the Internet. By clicking on Internet, you can see its subsectors. Click on any one, and you can see stock-performance charts of all the companies in that subsector. To magnify any chart, left-click it. You can also change features of the chart to see various data displayed.

3DStockCharts
www.3dstockcharts.com
This site offers three-dimensional charts showing prices, number of shares, and other data for the order books of electronic communication networks (ECNs) such as Island and Archipelago. Certain trading information is also available from the Instinet ECN.

Internet-Investment Sites

CBS Marketwatch
www.cbsmarketwatch.com/news/current/netdaily
A roundup of Net news stories.

Internet Stock Report
www.internetnews.com
News about internet stocks and industry trends. Links to other Internet-oriented sites. Provides Internet stock quotes.

Internet World Online
www.internetworld.com
News about companies, trends, new products, and comings and goings of key people within the industry. The site includes a calendar of industry events.

Red Herring
www.herring.com
A technology news site, with a heavy dose of Internet information.

Robertson Stephens
www.internetstocks.com
This site features industry trends and company news from Internet analysts at the investment firm Robertson Stephens. Reports are organized by Internet sectors.

The Standard
www.thestandard.com
News and analysis about Internet companies and industry trends from a widely followed news source. The site's metrics section offers features and graphics explaining and illustrating trends. A search engine lets you look for data and analysis by subject headings or prepackaged topics. You can check for developments in specific sectors of the Internet. Or you can look up news and data for individual companies.

Wired News
www.wired.com
Site that focuses on news about the digital world. Its sister site, *HotWired* (www.hotwired.com), reports on web technology and culture.

Glossary

12b-1 fee An annual fee charged by some mutual funds to pay for marketing and distribution. The fee is taken directly from fund assets, which reduces the return you get as a shareholder. (See *expense ratio.*)

Active management A strategy that requires managers to choose investments using their judgment. In contrast, passive management involves selecting investments to match a preexisting list or index. Active managers rely on research, computer models, market predictions, screening by criteria, experience, and other subjective or objective tools. The goal is usually to maximize a fund's performance. (See *passive management.*)

Annual report A corporation's annual statement of financial operations, provided to shareholders and potential investors. These are typically glossy, colorful publications. Annual reports include a balance sheet, income statement, auditor's report, and description of a company's operations. The Securities and Exchange Commission (SEC) requires that publicly traded companies file a more detailed annual report called a Form 10-K.

Likewise, a mutual fund's annual report explains how the fund has been doing. The fund's investments are listed, showing how much of each the fund owned as of the specified date. Also, each stock's industry is identified, and the portion of the fund's money in each industry is broken out. Typically, a letter from the fund group's chairman or president analyzes the fund's performance. This message discusses such things as how the stock market and the overall economy affected the fund's holdings. (Some funds are more detailed and candid than others.) Finally, the report presents the fund's financial highlights, summarizing details about such data as fund expenses, assets and liabilities, investment performance, and turnover ratio. Some details of the report focus on the preceding 12 months. Comparable analysis in a *semiannual report* looks at the previous six months.

ARPANET Acronym for Advanced Research Projects Agency Network. This computer network dating from the late 1960s is the Internet's ancestor. It was supported by the U.S. Defense Department. Eventually, it was opened to nonmilitary users doing defense-related research and then to other researchers.

B2B The nickname for business-to-business electronic commerce (e-commerce) or commerce conducted via the Internet. (See *e-commerce*.) The term also refers to a sector of the Internet industry.

B2C The nickname for business-to-consumer e-commerce. The term also refers to a sector of the Internet industry.

Back load (or back-end load) Commission that an investor may have to pay when he or she sells shares in a mutual fund. (See *load*.)

Bandwidth The amount of information that a network's circuits can carry. Bandwidth is measured in *bits per second*. A bit is the smallest piece of information that computers can process. Most network devices usually have capacity (*bandwidth*) in thousands of bits (kilobits) or millions of bits (megabits) per second. The more bandwidth you have, the faster you can receive data and the faster you can download text and images online.

Bond A bond is a loan to a borrower. That borrower can be a corporation or a government body like a city, state, or school system. The borrower promises to repay the loan itself (the *principal*) as well as pay interest for use of your money. Unlike stock, a bond does not represent ownership of the company. It's simply an IOU from the borrower to you. Its principal can grow or shrink.

Broadband Any type of telecommunications transmission whose bandwidth capacity is greater than a standard voice telephone line. Examples of broadband include a cable television coaxial cable, digital subscriber line, and fiber-optic cable. (See *digital subscriber line.*)

Browser Software that lets you navigate the Internet. It enables you to see and hear things on the Web, such as text, graphics, sound, and video. Two popular examples are Netscape Navigator and Microsoft Internet Explorer.

Build out The process of constructing the Internet's infrastructure.

Bulletin board A feature of many financial web sites, where people can post and read messages about companies and trends.

Capital gain Profit you make when you sell shares of a mutual fund, company stock, or bond for more than you paid. A *long-term capital gain* is your profit on the sale of securities you've owned more than a year. A *short-term capital gain* is your profit on the sale of securities owned one year or less.

Cash equivalent Investments that are easily convertible into cash and extremely unlikely to change value in the short-term. Examples include money market funds and Treasury bills.

Chat room A feature of many financial web sites, where people can read messages about companies and trends and type a message in response. The messages and responses appear onscreen in the order they are received, showing the electronic conversation's give-and-take.

Content Term for material on a web site, such as news or music. Content providers are organizations, often other than the site's host, that create the material. The term also refers to the content-provider sector of the Internet industry.

Cyberspace Slang term that refers to the Internet. *Cyber-* is used as a prefix to denote an activity done on the Internet or an Internet-related concept. For example, *cybercommerce* refers to business conducted over the Internet.

Domain Name of a network or computer system connected to the Internet, which is indicated in an e-mail address after the @ sign. A domain ends with an abbreviation telling you its type. For example, *.com* stands for commercial and *.gov* for government.

Dot-com company A company that offers goods or services on the Internet. To many people, the phrase refers only to B2C firms that sell exclusively through the Net. But the term also generally includes web firms that sell to other businesses, and it includes both B2C and B2B enterprises that sell offline as well.

DSL Acronym for digital subscriber line, which is a high-speed Internet access technology offered by phone companies and others. It is a competitor to other access technologies, such as high-speed cable-modem service. DSL is much faster than dialup modem access and about as fast as cable-modem service.

Despite using regular copper telephone lines, DSL's high bandwidth enables it to carry video, audio, and 3-D images as well as voice and data. The data part of the access is always on; your modem does not need to dial any numbers for connection to the Internet. The technology also lets you use a single line for voice and data, eliminating the need and cost for a second phone line.

In contrast, cable-modem access slows as more of your neighbors go online at the same time. That's because you and your neighbors are sharing the cable's bandwidth.

DSL has drawbacks, however. You often must live within about two miles of a phone company's central office that is appropriately equipped to obtain access. Also, phone companies have a reputation for poor installation and maintenance. And hookups for multiple personal computers in a home are reputedly difficult and costly.

Earnings per share The portion of a company's profits allocated to each outstanding share of common stock. (See *profit.*)

E-commerce Short-hand for electronic commerce, referring to business conducted through the Internet.

EDGAR The initials stand for the Securities and Exchange Commission's Electronic Data Gathering and Retrieval site. That's the online access point for filings companies are required to submit to the SEC, which is the U.S. government's watchdog over the investment industry. You can find everything from mutual fund prospectuses to corporate quarterly earnings reports.

E-mail Electronic mail, which is sent between networked computers.

Enabling technology Computers, software, associated devices, and standing equipment used by any aspect of the Internet. This term is basically synonymous with *infrastructure*. (See *infrastructure.*)

E-tail Short-hand for electronic retail, referring to retail business conducted through the Internet.

Expense ratio A fee that pays for a mutual fund's operating expenses. A fund may levy an expense ratio whether or not it charges a sales commission or load. An expense ratio includes management fees, administrative fees, and any 12b-1 fees. It is stated as the percentage of a portfolio's average net assets used to pay its annual expenses. For example, the average stock mutual fund charges an expense ratio of about 1.4 percent. For Internet funds the average is about 1.9 percent, according to Lipper, Inc. The return you get on a fund as a shareholder is reduced by the amount of the expense ratio.

Fiber optics Technology that sends telecommunications or computer information though thin flexible glass (or another transparent material like plastic) in the form of pulses of light. Since the pulses can be sent long distances with little loss of light, the technology is very useful for long-haul communications.

Fixed-income investment An investment, such as a bond or money-market fund, that pays a specified interest rate.

Front load (or front-end load) Commission that an investor may have to pay when he or she buys shares in a mutual fund. (See *load.*)

Graphical user interface A system that lets a user make a computer perform tasks by pointing to small pictures or symbols (called *icons*) on the computer screen and clicking with a mouse button.

http Standing for *Hypertext Transfer Protocol*, http is a common system used to send *HTML documents* on the World Wide Web. It is the first portion of all URL addresses on the World Wide Web; it precedes the *www* part of the address. It consists of a set of rules for exchanging files between computers. Those files often contain references to other files, with a built-in request to automatically switch or *link* you to that file elsewhere.

Technically, this is the part of an Internet address that tells you what computer language must be used to reach a specified web site.

Incubator A company that provides a sheltered setting for startup firms, helping them survive and develop while they are at their youngest and most vulnerable. The host company may provide financing and help arrange further funding. It may also help its brood firms to network, share ideas, and conduct business with each other and outside corporations and agencies. In addition, the host may offer pooled services, which the startups can share, reducing their respective overhead costs.

Infrastructure The machinery, standing equipment, and software used by the Internet's countless computers to operate and interact. This Net skeleton consists of such things as computers, software, modems, microchips, copper telephone cables, fiber-optic network equipment, and wireless transmission towers. The term also refers to a sector of the Internet industry.

Internet A network of computer networks, which was created in the late 1960s. The *Net*, as people often call it, lets a user at any one computer exchange information with other computers on the system.

Internet service provider Often called an *ISP*, this is an organization that provides most members of the general public with access to the Net. An ISP, which is typically a private company, sells access through networks of local phone numbers. Alternatively, many people get onto the Internet through a computer that's part of a participating network, such as at their work place or a research institution.

IPO Acronym for initial public offering, which refers to a corporation's first offering of stock to the public. An IPO is typically an opportunity for investors, including venture capitalists, who already own stock in the company to profit handsomely. That's because shares often are priced higher than they were previously, in anticipation of the company's future growth.

Local Area Network A LAN is a group of computers linked in a network. The computers generally are located near each other, as in a business office. Connecting them lets people on that network all have access to common sources of information, such as a company's sales records or accounting system. (See *storage area network*.)

Load A commission on the purchase or sale of mutual-fund shares.

Low-load fund A fund that charges a sales commission of 3.5 percent or less when you buy shares. (See *load*.)

Market leader A company with one of the largest shares of all the businesses in its field.

Microprocessor An integrated circuit that can "understand" and use instructions from a computer program. A microprocessor is the engine that runs a computer.

Modem A device that connects two computers (or other digital device) over a telephone line. It works by converting outgoing digital signals from a computer to analog signals, which travel over ordinary telephone lines. A modem at the receiving end reconverts incoming analog signals into digital data for the second computer.

Mutual fund A bundle of investments that is managed by one or more investment professionals. The managers pool your money with other peoples' and use it to buy investments such as stocks, bonds, and other securities. When you invest in a fund, you purchase shares in the fund rather than the underlying securities. The price of mutual fund shares is determined basically by dividing the number of shares into the market value of what it owns.

Networking The design and construction of hardware, software, support equipment, and rules for use, which together let people communicate through a system of interconnected computers.

New Economy A catchall term commonly used to refer to companies engaged in Internet-based activities. In contrast, *Old Economy* refers to companies not using the Internet much if at all.

Online Being connected to the Internet. *Offline* means not being connected. The terms are commonly used to describe whether business or other activities are being conducted by way of the Internet.

No-load fund A mutual fund that charges no sales commission or load. Even a no-load fund, however, can charge a fee called an *expense ratio* to pay for operating expenses. (See *load*.)

Passive management (See *active management*.)

PC-centric A system based on personal computers. For example, software that affects the operations of the PC in which it is installed is PC-centric. In contrast, software that focuses on the operation of network equipment or on the operation of individual computers once they are connected to the Internet is Net-centric, Web-centric, or network-centric.

Personal digital assistant Often referred to as a *PDA*, this is a handheld, wireless-telecommunications device that is used to send, receive, and store data, messages, and miscellaneous information. These appliances provide a popular way to carry an updatable calendar or address book, and to receive brief bulletins about investments. Increasingly, PDAs can access the Internet. You can commonly read messages displayed on a liquid display crystal screen. And you can input information by way of a small keypad.

Portal A World Wide Web site that gives people access to content and other sites. However, a portal is not the same thing as an Internet service provider (ISP), which is a company that provides access to the Internet itself. Examples of portals that are familiar to the general Internet public are Yahoo!, Netscape, and America Online. Portals may provide free access or charge a fee. They also typically offer other attractions, such as e-mail, games, discussion groups, chat rooms, information resources like encyclopedias, and investment news and research. (See *Internet service provider*.)

Portfolio All of your individual investments—whether they are stocks, bonds, mutual funds, or some other security—as a group. For example, if you are a member of a 401(k) plan, all of the investments in your account are your portfolio in the plan.

Portfolio manager The person in charge of a mutual fund's investment decisions.

Price/earnings ratio The *p/e ratio*, as it's commonly called, is a ratio of a stock's price per share divided by its annual per-share earnings. It is a popular formula for measuring how expensive a company's earnings are. It translates stock price into a multiple of earnings. For example, if a company's earnings per share this year total $1.50 and its share price is $12, its p/e ratio is eight. Investors would say the company is selling or trading at eight times earnings or "a multiple of 8." (See *earnings per share* and *profit*.)

Profit A company's profit is its net income, which is what remains of its revenue after all expenses, including taxes, have been paid.

Prospectus Technically a legal document, a prospectus describes a mutual fund's investment strategy, goals, risks, sales commissions and operating costs, performance history, and manager.

Pure-play Often used as an adjective to indicate that an investment like a mutual fund focuses on the Internet. For example, StockJungle.com Pure Play Internet Fund even uses it in its name. An individual company is generally deemed to be a pure Internet firm, or a *pure play*, if more than half of its revenues are due to doing business on or because of the Internet. Some investors, though, reserve the term for businesses that derive their revenues exclusively through or due to the Net. Likewise, a pure-play fund would be one that invests more than half of its money (or all of it) in Internet-oriented businesses.

Quarter One of the four three-month periods into which each fiscal year is divided for accounting and various performance reporting and tracking purposes.

Rate of return Rate of return describes an investment's growth (or loss). It includes how much a stock, bond, or mutual fund's shares rise or fall in price. It also consists of any interest, dividends, or other income paid by the investment. The price change plus income is stated as a percentage of your initial investment or the value of the investment at the start of a specified period, such as the calendar year.

Relative price strength A measurement of a stock's price performance relative to other stocks.

Risk The potential for losing money or not making money on an investment. Generally, there are four major types of risk: business risk, which is the danger that a company could fail or run unprofitably; interest risk, which is the hazard caused by the price of money (including money you or a company would need to borrow) rising; market risk, which is the possibility that larger economic, social, or political forces could harm a company's ability to conduct business; and inflation risk, which is the peril posed by the erosion of your money's purchasing power.

Risk tolerance The amount of danger or volatility you can tolerate in your investments. It will vary according to such variables as your circumstances, age, income, financial resources, and amount of time before you need to use your money.

Router A computer dedicated to directing or routing data over networks. It's the traffic cop of the Information Superhighway. Routers are at the heart of the Internet's thousands of networks. A router chooses a path across a network for the data it handles. Its job is to make sure data gets from one network to another. Each router handles an enormous volume of data.

Its function differs from that of computers called *servers*, which store information and software programs and dish them out to people using other computers.

Search engine A service that helps you find material online. You use one by typing in words or phrases, known as *keywords*. The tool then finds and lists web sites that contain the information you're seeking. Some fancy search engines have started to offer more services and content of their own, making themselves into *portals*.

Semiannual report (See *annual report*.)

Semiconductors A material that conducts electricity under some conditions but not others, making it a good building block for computer chips.

Server A computer that stores information and software programs and provides (or *serves*) them to people using other computers. A server is the host to groups of computers linked in a network. (See *router*.)

Stock Stock represents ownership of a corporation. Each share of stock is an individual portion of ownership. For example, if you own 100 shares of a company that has issued 100,000 shares, you own one-thousandth of the company. That's one-tenth of 1 percent. The price or value of shares can rise or fall.

Storage area network A high-speed network that serves as a staging (or, as its name suggests, storage) area for data that is used by a larger, more general network. It is basically a warehouse for the larger network, where data can be backed up, archived, or held in readiness for sharing. (See *local area network*.)

Tax-deferred Individual Retirement Accounts (IRAs), 401(k) plans, and similar retirement accounts provide temporary tax protection to investments. If those investments pay dividends or capital gains, you don't have to pay taxes on that income. Similarly, if you well shares at a profit but keep the proceeds inside the account, you won't owe tax. You only have to pay tax at your ordinary income-tax rate when you take money out of a tax-deferred account.

Time horizon The amount of time that you expect to hold an investment. Generally, the longer you plan to keep an investment before needing to sell it to raise cash, the more short-term volatility you can tolerate.

URL URL stands for *Uniform Resource Locator*, which is a file's address on the Internet. The URL contains the name of the program or set of rules needed to access the file. It also includes the file's domain name, which tells you its home computer or host, and other information you need to pin down the file's exact location on the Web.

Virtual private network A private data network that uses public telecommunication infrastructure. A *VPN* gives a company the capabilities of a private network that utilizes lines only that company can use, but at lower cost by avoiding the overhead burden of private telecom lines.

Web Short-hand for *World Wide Web*. (See *World Wide Web*.)

Web site A web site is a group of related World Wide Web files or pages, which can be reached from a starting file called a home page. (See *World Wide Web*.)

Wireless Telecommunications relying mainly on radio signals rather than ground wires. Cell phones, pagers, and personal digital assistants are familiar users of wireless technology. The term also refers to a sector of the Internet industry.

World Wide Web The World Wide Web is a major part of the Internet, consisting of a network of computers using hypertext-linked databases and files. Developed in 1989 by Tim Berners-Lee, a British computer scientist, the Web consists of software programs and rules governing the way that text and pictures appear onscreen. A key feature is its built-in ability to link sites anywhere on this vast network and allow users to go easily from one to another.

Yield The current interest and dividend income from a bond or fund. Yield is measured and expressed as a percentage of a bond's face value or a fund's net asset value. Typically, it is based on income over the past 30 days, and it is annualized or stated in terms of what it would be at its existing pace for the coming year.

Index